YOUR LIFE IS A BLESSING...SO LIVE IT THAT WAY!!!!!

How I grew into the loving spirit I have become and how we all can become the best people we were born to be.

BY JOEL DEX GOOR

Copyright © 2014 NOVEMBER BY JOEL DEX GOOR
All rights reserved. This book or any portion thereof
may not be reproduced or used in any manner whatsoever
without the express written permission of the publisher
except for the use of brief quotations in a book review.
Printed in the United States of America

PLEASE CONTACT ME THROUGH MY BLOG:
"YOUR LIFE IS A BLESSING SO LIVE IT THAT WAY.COM"

COVER PHOTO: ID 12987365 © David Morrison | Dreamstime.com
5 AFFIRMATION STONES.

First Printing, 2014

ISBN :: **ISBN-13: 978-0692341490**
(Joel Dex Goor)

ISBN-10: 0692341498

YOUR LIFE IS A BLESSING...SO LIVE IT THAT WAY!!!!!

How I grew into the loving spirit I have become and how we all can become the best people we were born to be.

BY JOEL DEX GOOR

I DEDICATE MY FIRST BOOK TO ALL THE BLESSINGS IN MY LIFE:

GOD AND HIS LOVING ANGELS BOTH ON EARTH AND IN HEAVEN

THE UNIVERSE AND THE POWERS THAT BE IN THIS LIFE AND TO ALL THAT IS GOOD PURE AND INNOCENT IN THE WORLD OF LOVE …I SAY "THANK YOU."

MY LOVING MOTHER "MARCIA" WHO GAVE ME "THE GIFT OF LIFE"

MY LOVING SISTER: SHERRY (MY BEST FRIEND)

MY LOVING NEPHEW JASON ALEXANDER (THE GREAT)

MY LOVING NEPHEW MATTHEW TYLER (THE TERRIFIC)

THEIR DAD JAY

OUR BELOVED PUPPY DOODLE: "AUTUMN"

OUR LOVING UNCLE (MORRIS) RED AGED 92 GOD BLESS HIM

IN LOVING TRIBUTE: MY FAVORITE GREAT GRANDMOTHER SOPHIE AN ANGEL IN HEAVEN

IN LOVING TRIBUTE: MY GRANDPARENTS WHO ARE ANGELS IN HEAVEN: GRANDPA SAM AND NANNY JEANNE

IN LOVING TRIBUTE: MY FAVORITE AUNT AN ANGEL IN HEAVEN "AUNT ROSIE"

AND

IN LOVING TRIBUTE TO OUR BELOVED PUPPY: BOIZYBEST, AN ANGEL IN HEAVEN

I DEDICATE MY FIRST BOOK:

TO LOVING FRIENDS WHO HAVE BEEN MY "ROCK" THROUGHOUT MY LIFE ALONG WITH THE AFOREMENTIONED

GREAT SCHOOL TEACHER ROSEANN FIORE/ HUSBAND MICHAEL E. FIORE

GREAT LOVING BEST FRIENDS: PAULA AND ERIC SHOSTACK.

TRUE LOVING FRIENDS CONCETTA GRILLO/ HER BELOVED SON: NICHOLAS LOVINGLY NICKNAMED "BABY ANGEL" / YOUNG EARTH ANGEL

CARMELA AND VINNY ACCARDO AND FAMILY

MR. NICHOLAS AND MRS. ROSETTA GRILLO

TRUE LOVING FRIEND LORI PIZZARELLI AND HER FAMILY

MY FRIEND, BROTHER, SPIRIT, KEN ZHAO AND HIS LOVING WIFE JASMINE

MY FRIEND, BROTHER, SPIRIT, AAMIR QURESHI AND HIS LOVING FAMILY

LOVING SOULS: YANICK MICHEL / PASTOR MICHEL: GOD IS GOOD…ALL THE TIME

WORLD TREASURE: GLORIA DANZIGER WHO HAS HELPED ME MOVE FORWARD IN LIFE

I DEDICATE MY FIRST BOOK:

"YOUR LIFE IS A BLESSING...SO LIVE IT THAT WAY!!!!!"

AND ALL MY FUTURE BOOKS TO YOU THE READER. I HOPE MY BOOKS WITH HELP YOU LIVE MORE MEANINGFUL LIVES.

I HOPE THEY ALLOW YOU TO BECOME MORE DEEPER, MORE LOVING AND MORE COMPASSIONATE PEOPLE.

I HOPE MY WRITING WILL HELP YOU TO SEE YOUR LIFE IN A BETTER LIGHT THEN PERHAPS BEFORE AND FOR ALL WHO ENCIRCLE YOUR LIFE AND WORLD AS WELL.

THANK YOU FOR BUYING THIS BOOK!!!!

ACKNOWLEDGEMENT PAGE:

I also want to say THANK YOU to a few more people who in some form, Large and small, gave me help, guidance, as well as to help me figure things out in regards to the next step after writing my book. I must say thank you to them as well. Being grateful and acknowledging that gratefulness and thankfulness is so important.

Thank you Dear God, Your loving angels, the universe and the powers that be. Thank you so much!!!!

Thank you to my beautiful loving mother, Marcia N. My beautiful loving sister Sherry. My loving nephew Jason who helped me with different aspects of the book process, thank you. My loving nephew Matthew who lives with Autism. Thank you for teaching me so much about Love. Autumn our new beloved Southern Belle Pooch.

Wonderful loving friends. Gloria D. Concetta, Lori, Yanick, Ken, and AAmir, you all mean the world to me and forever live inside my heart.

RoseAnn Fiore my school teacher who taught me and helped me so much along the way with her Husband, Michael E. Fiore, thank you so much and God bless you both. My best friend and buddy Eric, a special needs person who taught me so much about friendship and kindness and his mom Paula

These new friends and angels came through social media. Megan Talbot who helped me with a piece of writing after the book had been completed as I thought I was going to try sending it out to a book publisher, but plans changed and I self-published instead.

Thank you to Melissa Meadows for giving me some very helpful advice, as well as introducing me to your friend who had already "self-published her book: Medea Yorba author of "DARCY'S LAST PROMISE." Thank you Medea!!!! You gave me bits and pieces of advice, enough to get me started and get me on the road to being a self-published author. I'm forever grateful. Thank you to all FACEBOOK friends as well, such as: Loving spirit Jenny Harper LeBel who introduced me to some other loving spirits such Glenn G. McGee, and Barbara Saefke. Shari Sacolick a FACEBOOK friend who became a fan of my writing, as well as Pamela Pena Jaffa Quartararo another wonderful fan. Friends James O Edwards Alba Cerrone and Prayer group friend Sherry Stoll. Friends Karen Ruiz, and Maximilian Mendoza a great friend I've known for 20 years now long distance. Thank you Rebecca Russo, Sheri Wertkin (Kron), and Gail Goldstein Gill and wonderful co-worker of many years Ghazala Chaudhry.

We can never have enough loving fans who appreciate our work. Thank you to all my wonderful FACEBOOK friendships. If I forgot your name here, I am twice blessed and would lovingly add your name in my second book. I am grateful for all your friendships.

Thank you again for all the 'LIKES," on my fanpage:

"MY HAPPINESS, GRATITUDE AND APPRECIATION PAGE"

1, 900 "LIKES" as of this printing

Thank you, Thank you, Thank You. Much Love to all. May this book be a success and when it does become one, I have only you the readers, my audience to thank and I do.

Please find me on social media:

FACEBOOK FRIENDS PAGE: Joel Dex Goor

FACEBOOK FANPAGE: "MY HAPPINESS, GRATITUDE AND APPRECIATION PAGE"

TWITTER: @JoelDexGoor

FACEBOOK FANPAGE: "YOUR LIFE IS A BLESSING SO LIVE IT THAT WAY!!!"

TABLE OF CONTENTS

DEDICATION/ ACKNOWLEDGEMENTS/ AUTHOR CONTACT PAGES...

INTRODUCTION.... I

CHAPTER 1: OUR FAMILIES AND OUR FRIENDSHIPS....1

CHAPTER 2: HAPPINESS, GRATITUDE AND APPRECIATION....25

CHAPTER 3: A WORLD WITH MORE KINDNESS AND COMPASSION....47

CHAPTER 4: CARING ABOUT OTHER PEOPLE & OURSELVES....66

CHAPTER 5: LEARNING, GROWING, AND KNOWING....76

CHAPTER 6: IF WE LIVE OUR LIVES WITH INTEGRITY OUR LIVES WILL SHINE EVER SO BRIGHTLY....93

CHAPTER 7: CULTURE, RELIGION AND SPIRITUALITY....107

CHAPTER 8: RACISM SHOULD NEVER EXIST...124

CHAPTER 9: WORLD PEACE AND HUMANITY....135

CHAPTER 10: VOLUNTEERING AND HELPING OTHERS....153

CHAPTER 11: RESPECTING OTHERS, AS WE WOULD WANT OTHERS TO RESPECT US....168

CHAPTER 12: OUR TIME ON THIS EARTH AND OUR PURPOSE IN LIFE....183

CHAPTER 13: THE GIFTS AND STRUGGLES OF OUR LIVES....208

CHAPTER 14: WITH LIFE, COMES THE SADNESS OF LOSS....227

CHAPTER 15: THE IMPORTANT THINGS THAT MATTER.....244
EPILOGUE....260 ABOUT THE AUTHOR...264

INTRODUCTION

Everyone is put upon the earth with a purpose and a calling. Through deep searching, I have discovered mine. If I so choose as well to hear, honor and follow it then I will hopefully have enriched my life and our world too. To have transformed it to a more loving world, a more peaceful world, a gentler world, then I sincerely hope my life will have made a "profound," statement. I feel and know my purpose and my calling is to be that of a writer and a humanitarian: a healer through words and a healer through my actions. Helping others is what I am here to do. This is my purpose and my calling and my reason for living.

Joyfully, I arise to the occasion to always be focusing on the needs of others whether it be a family member or friend, a co-worker, a patient at work, or a stranger on the street. I choose to think of humanity first. I hope you do as well.

In all that I do and wherever I go, I ask, "How I can be of service to others and make the lives of others more enriched?" "How can I be of service and where can I give aid to those in need?" These are some of the questions I ask of myself and encourage others to ask of themselves as well. We should never rest until the questions are answered and we can accomplish the work at hand which is always making the lives of others in some form easier, happier, and more joyous because all of us deserve it as spirits who walk the earth.

How we can be of service to the elderly, or teach and embrace the magical gifts of children or show love to everyone else sandwiched in between? One thing I know for sure is, there is one constant in all of our lives and that is that we all want and need the same things: love and kindness, a happy life with good health, caring people in our lives and validation at any age that we matter to others.

Our lives are but a gift and a blessing that we need to respect and embrace. We all have our journeys to travel on with many different roads and crossroads and paths to follow. Some lives are long, full and vibrant and can live to 100 and beyond, while other people's lives can be just as full and vibrant doing what they need to do to make a contribution to the world and then their life as we know it is over in a mere 20 or 30 years in this earthly form. Some are like a supernova star, their lives shine brightly and are gone quickly, such as that of 13 year old peacemaker Mattie J. T. Stepanek. He and others have returned to full spirit and on to their next path or journey of existence in that realm of life.

Although we do have faith that we may go beyond this life into something better, this may be our only chance to make a difference in this worldly realm and we need to give it all we've got. That difference is not for one person or just ourselves, it is for all people, because when we all benefit we all succeed and we all win. The only winning prospects are win-win situations. All parties go away feeling great about the outcome of any situation and it lasts. I want to be one person to make that difference in the lives of one, or many lives. I believe at the gut level this is what we all want which is to win at this thing called, "life." This is the place where God would have me be and these are the causes that God would have me be working to help heal. Looking at the needs of others and how I can help to heal them in whatever form would best be for their benefit is the way I want to help humanity.

The best way I know I can complete the world and contribute to the world is in my humanitarian efforts or in my healing words as a writer, both are places my gifts can best be of service to others in this world.

If this happened to be the only book I wrote the world has chosen to embrace and believe in, I hope the message or messages I would want them to take from this is to know that I cared about others as a loving "citizen of the world." I wanted to help others and be there for others and show that someone does and did care about them and validate their existence. I lived my life showing them they were important just for being alive. I wanted to brighten their lives to push them in the direction of greater heights. The light that was in them shown brightly because the same light they had I did as well and we recognized it in each other.

My first book is a spiritual and inspirational series of essays and of quotes. It is a journey of our collective lives through my life experience. My chapters begin with the essays and end with the many quotes that I have conceived in relation to these 15 essays. I hope you find these quotes profoundly inspirational and thought provoking to help our world to realize our truest value; as well as the essays, which precede them. I write to change lives; first my own and then to inspire others to find the best within themselves. When we find the best within ourselves we can then be the example to and for others to find the best within themselves and that is what this book sets forth in doing.

I hope in my book I can share with you what helped me and led me to become the person I have become, the human spirit I was always destined to be. I hope all humanity can gain some insight and wisdom through what I hope to share so you can discover the best within you and then share it with the world. We all have the right and the capacity for greatness, we just have to allow ourselves the permission to discover it and extend it to the world, because the world is waiting for us to be a blessing upon it. In each essay and along with my quotes, I share with you, my reader what led up to my living with what I hope are sincere ideals we all can believe in, one form or another. The people, the situations, the places that showed me what is important and how to best affect a human life in my thoughts and in my actions are what this book is about and what I want to share with the world. I am no different than anyone else in that I want to find my purpose and calling and start the work of doing it. We all want and need validation that we can achieve anything of value in life. We want to know it for ourselves and pass it on to others searching in their own lives for something deeply important and meaningful. This is something all of us can do to become which is a society of more generous human spirits walking the planet with purpose.

    We as individuals shine when we all shine. A remembered statement paraphrased from 'A Course in Miracles' says "All of us are special and none of us are special." The course is one way of spiritual practice that I embrace and follow. All of us are important but none is more important than anyone else. When we see people shining in their lives this should be an awakening to us that we can shine too in all we do.

    With this book, I hope to inspire others to live better lives. Each day we read the papers and see the evening news on TV and we see so many parts of the world filled with human tragedy and devastation beyond anyone has a right to be a part of. There are war torn areas along with earthquakes, tornadoes, hurricanes and mudslides, which can swallow up lives and the ones who survive, have their homes and life belongings taken leaving them only to rebuild. The ones left behind had to try to mend the shattered pieces of their lives. Nevertheless, it is so important to always remember and never forget that with all the horrific tragedy in the world which I would never invalidate, there is so much more beauty then could ever be tragedy if we just look and embrace the meaningful a little more.

    We have the gift of our families which include the blessings of babies and children who we wish upon them health and happiness. The comfort of a warm, safe, and loving home with solid jobs and solid incomes when we are blessed to have them it is important to behold them with grace and gratitude. Having friends that care about our welfare and will help us and we them when needed is what is important. Having a few nice things not a whole lot of "stuff," is also important because we don't need a lot of "stuff," to have meaningful lives. Helping others in need brings us up to our highest selves, leading us to become the best people we were meant to be. We all have this ability of becoming the best people we can if we so choose to embrace this fact and do the necessary work to get there. Why would we not want to embrace the best within us? Why would we not go out and help someone else? It is so easy and the rewards are priceless beyond words, beyond measure. Everyone wins and no one loses. Sometimes we can go out looking for someone to help and other times they find us. The universe knows what direction to go in and bring people together. When we show the universe how we treat others does the universe pay that back in kind. Hopefully, it will be for good and not for bad.

God is the Creator and we are the co-creators of our lives. Whatever our destiny is, we can make the choice to do our best and become the best in whatever area that we so choose or that so chooses us in our God-given talents. Whether we write romantic love poems, play the sweet sounds of a violin, or painting a huge mural, and even building a house for others to live in, find what can make us shine and go express that gift. We can build great pyramids, and climb majestic mountain tops if we so desire. There is no limit to what we can do and achieve in our lives if we so choose to and go ahead and pursue it.

What may seem large and looming to one may not seem so hard to accomplish for another. Each of us sees things differently from a different perspective. I would never go out into the woods, or hiking or any outdoor type of situations. I am more a creature of comfort, inside my home with heat in the winter and air conditioning in the summer, a nice warm bed with a computer, TV and food, while others love the outdoors and are alive when it comes to hiking and traveling in the woods or mountain tops. Each needs to do things that make them grow and/or feel great about themselves.

I feel through my own experience and for my life that the majestic mountain top is becoming a great writer and a great humanitarian in the way I define it as opposed to the way the world may define it. Writing that changes lives, and helping others so I can change a life, those are my purpose principles and definitions. Some may think that noble and admirable and others might think it Pollyanna. Either way it is what I am creating for my life and world. Each of us has that right and ability to do so. I am doing mine and I want and encourage others to search out and do theirs lovingly.

So, I hope each essay, thought, ideal, and quote in this book will excite you, inspire and/or give you food for thought in how one person has lived their life and how maybe you might live your life for the better in the way you see fit. I hope you will allow yourself to create your world the way you need to in order to pass it along to others for future generations to come. They deserve it and we owe it to them as we owe it to ourselves. Make it a great life for one and for all and please live it with some sort of grace and gratitude. My wish is that I can be a conduit in some form to help you reach that place of greatness in your life. Much love and magical blessings on our time spent together.

Chapter 1:

OUR FAMILIES AND OUR FRIENDSHIPS

Our family and our friendships if we have been blessed are the ones who will sustain us in this life. They are there for us through the wonderful times where life resembles the sparkle in a jewel, and as well as the times where life can be a constant struggle and uphill battle and darkness seems to invade our souls. We are there for them in the same way and we want to give and be there for them as any true loving person would be. We know this to be true and we should live our lives with that thought in mind.

Be a friend and you will have a friend. It sounds easy and it is, but we just have to want it and then pursue it. In this life to be alone without anyone is a deep sadness, wouldn't you agree? The truth is we need people in our lives that we can go to when the chips are down, when the world seems to be against us for the moment and which in our minds seems like it could last forever. We need them to hug us, love us and tell us that, "this too shall pass," or "what you are feeling now is normal, and things will turn out okay."

When we are up we want others to tell us "how great we did and how well we can be better still if needed." We need people in our lives who tell us we can climb the highest mountaintops and we can and will make it, if not now, then eventually. Positive energy is flowing from them to us, from us to them. This is something that we all need no matter what culture, generation or part of the globe we originate from we all need basic ingredients in our lives in order to survive and thrive and these include: love, kindness, friendship, forgiveness and compassion. When we have those ingredients in the pot whatever that could go wrong in our lives will hopefully not be so severe in its undertaking when our loved ones of family and friends are there to help us get through it. Yet there are people in this world who seem to have no one. They are lacking in family and quality friendships. This is sad and I believe that the best way to help others who don't have friends or any family to speak of is to become their friend and so they do not feel so alone, unwanted and unloved. We must be that vessel of peace and love for each other.

On the last episode of "The Mary Tyler Moore Show," Mary Richards answered the profound question about "what is a family?" I believe it pertains to friendship as well and that these people exist in our lives because "they make us feel less lonely and they make us feel loved," Mary Richards whose words I paraphrased and I believe it rings true, and *that* is the meaning of our family and our friendships.

There may be times when those relationships with our family and friends appear sour and we fight and yell at one another, but once we can get past those sour moments we find the sweetness and great fruits that truly do exist, which get overshadowed and hidden in what should be real and genuine. They are the ones who should sustain us, take care of us and nurture the good in us to live our very best lives. They give to us and we make sure we give back to them and others. When we do allow this to happen we feel great inside and it will reflect back into the world and in all our relationships.

What saddens my heart is when our families fight to the extent that no one is happy and hate and sadness fill our hearts. When instead of having an easy heart it is replaced by a heavy one.

In the past, I have had unloving arguments with a family member and it was not a healthy relationship. It was filled with negativity and disrespectful dialogue on both sides. We both fought and would hold a grudge that would last for the longest time before we would start to speak to each other again. However, in truth grudges were not and are not healthy. Through the years, that negative and unloving dialogue would sneak back into our way with each other and nothing would be resolved but the same old patterns would return. I had promised myself that after close to four decades though prayer, meditation, spirituality and forgiveness to not go back to the way we had fought in the past. It was unhealthy on anyone's part. I knew that I had to change my thinking and my own attitude to restore and make the relationship a more loving one. Gandhi said, "You must be the change you want to see in the world." I believe also that we must be the change we want to see in others. This is not to say that the other party does not need to change their thinking and attitude, but we can only change our own thinking and actions toward others. If we are caring and loving, the changes in others will be caring and loving as well. If we are disrespectful and unloving to others it will return back to us. It is as simple as that.

    I also believe that sometimes as we all do we live with past hurts from our childhood where we blame our parents and others for them. As we grow and hopefully mature we get past the hurts by coming to terms with them and not blaming others such as our parents for them. They did the best in times of constant struggle to raise their family when times were tough. We eventually learn like I did to make peace with past hurts or hopes of having things another way instead of the way they truly were. Once we become adults we become in charge of our own lives and need to learn or teach ourselves what might not have been able to be taught to us for whatever reason under the sun. Math and money were never my strong point, and now that I am mature enough I can teach myself what I need to know about math, and money or not, it is always my choice as the adult.

Once I laid the past to rest what I did then which was to create a better relationship with my family member and I found it was the best move I could have made. Because once a relationship is gone and leaves this world there is no turning back. All those years that may have been wasted are now restored to its proper potential. My family member and I now have a wonderful adult relationship. We can now enjoy each others company and have incredible conversations about life and at the same time we can laugh till it hurts watching I Love Lucy, Maude, The Jefferson's and The Golden Girls among others.

If we as individuals can get past the hurts and pain and let it go we will find what truly should exist which is that of wonderful relationships with our family members and others. We can take it further and have much healthier relationships with friends and other people including co-workers, as well as the people at the checkout of the local grocery store and yes, of course with complete strangers who are truly our brothers and sisters.

I have always said and believed since I have lived it one time or another that when we are on the outs with our parents, siblings, spouse or loved one that outside relationships can seem tarnished or just not right. They do not seem right because how can we be genuine to our friends, co-workers or whomever we know when the most important people in our lives are not speaking to us or us to them. All relationships can seem fake and phony with a cloud hanging over it when our relationships with our loved ones are strained and having lost its true meaning of what family is? These are the people who love us, make us feel wanted, needed and less alone, as Mary Richards said in essence. It is so true.

Of course, there are some relationships in our families that can never be healed and that we have to let them go in order for us to be healed as individuals if not collectively. Forgiveness is important, but at the same time if the relationship with a family member or friend is not salvageable it is important to let them go and heal the wounds of the past and then live our lives as best we can.

Friendships are another wonderful group of people to connect with and love. Our friends are the people that we can choose as opposed to our family members and if we choose friends that have the same values, interests and likes as we do, we then have the beginnings of a long lasting, beautiful and sacred friendship.

Friendships take on different levels and yet each can be special in its own way. Some friendships are casual, who we see from time to time and others who we hang out with more frequently. Some are just telephone friends. I had a friend whom I used to speak with on the telephone and when we run into each other in the neighborhood. We are both from different generations and yet we spent as much as two hours on the phone talking. We talked about everything from our favorite soap, "One Life To Live," to politics, life and family, etc.

We as friends are there for happy times such as a birthday, anniversary, or graduations, and sad times such as the passing of a loved one, or serious problem that only our friends can get us through. My friend Lori has brought me groceries when I was sick with bronchitis and Concetta another great friend has helped me when I was dealing with depression. I have good friends and I look for ways to pay them back. I believe that friendship is a two-way street, not tit-for-tat but by the beautiful concept of "giving and receiving." It is so important to be able to graciously live on both sides of the coin. It is a great feeling giving to others and we should never feel funny about receiving from others too.

    We seem only to have this one life to live and having the best relationships with our family and friends are so important. I am so blessed to have them with my mom, sister, nephews and loving family pet and many friends. Speaking with them, connecting and spending time with them and them with us is our most important opportunity for soul growth in relationships. These are the most important people in our lives and we should embrace them, and love them and by doing this we can make this great scary world seem less scary.

    I can sincerely say that having our family and our friends close by and near us makes living on this planet a more humbling and happy experience. Without sincere love in our lives, do we not feel short-changed and are we not missing something so powerful that is beyond this mortal world. Being alone with no one while we are here on this earth because of bitterness and a stone cold heart is simply no way to live. Will not everyone lose, and isn't life supposed to be a win-win situation? Even though life may seem unfair, we need to make our life a win-win proposition. It can be, we just need to stay connected to our family and our friends as well as others who serve a mighty purpose in our lives. Let all go which has no true meaning. Sadness and pain caused by someone to us or us to them, hate, and destruction just pulls us down to where everyone loses. However, if we show love, kindness, friendship, forgiveness and compassion to all who enter our lives and want to stay apart of our lives we will then look back on a life well lived and commented on by all who knew us by saying that our life was a "successful and well lived life."

In conclusion, both our family and our friendships are and can be the strongest bonds we make, the most loving ones we have and the ones that will take us through the toughest times and celebrate with us the tenderest of moments that life can bring with it. With all the cruelty that this world endures, all we have is each other and we need to be there for each other. So look at the family we have, the friendships we make and say a prayer and wish that it always be the blessing it can be and truly is...Amen.

"As the old adage goes "we can choose our friends, but not our family." I believe both are vitally important though. We need both family to help teach us the lessons we need to make it in the world and friends to tell our secrets to. Our families are there to give us food and shelter, love and foundation. Our friends are there to laugh with us and spend time with us and help us make peace out of the chaos that is in our lives sometimes. Our relationships with family and friends are so important, because both provide key ingredients in creating the people we are to become as we move through our lives. So let us do our best to make them work."

"Some of us have large families and some just have small ones. We should be thankful because there are some that have no family to speak of, no one to care for them or about them. They have no one to remember their birthday or a special moment in childhood, or even remember that they exist. Families large and small are important and we should be appreciative of what we have, when we have it."

"Some of us are blessed with the best parents, and some of us have not. The ones who have the best parents can grow into the best people we are capable of becoming. The ones who didn't have the best parents or family members can STILL come out on TOP and also be the BEST, because all HOPE is NOT lost. We just have to find some grasp of faith to hold on to and then go with that until we get to the places we need and were meant to be and then our lives will truly shine."

"Life is so very short and once our parents and grandparents, our aunts and uncles, or brothers and sisters leave us to return to heaven, that is it. So enjoy the experiences of life and time with them. Listen to their stories and embrace their love because this is essentially all we have. So I hope we can create beautiful loving memories and through this know that this is what families and friendships are all about, which is giving and receiving love."

"We need to be there for our families and our friends. We need to help nurture them when they are down and bring them back up again. We need to tell them they are right or wrong and they need to tell us the same things in return. It is not always easy but it is important to make sure we show up and are there for the people we love and who love us."

"Babies and children are the sweetness of the earth so nestle and love them and teach them well. If we raise them up to always keep their sweetness, they will bring it into their adulthood and a more sweet and loving world will exist."

Watch and enjoy children laugh and play and then take a lesson from them and we ourselves should be able to laugh and play each week as well, despite the responsibilities that seem to take the place of our own laughter and playtime that we all deserve to incorporate into our lives. Let us all learn to take time to smell the roses and appreciate what is most important and laughter and playtime will help us remember that."

"RESPECT THE RIGHTS OF OUR CHILDREN AND PROTECT OUR CHILDREN FROM EVIL IN THIS WORLD. ALWAYS WATCH OVER THEM, AND KNOW WHERE THEY ARE AT ALL TIMES. In this way we can ensure their safety and they will mature in healthy loving ways as all children should."

"Teach and inspire children to become what they dream and become who they most want to be. We also need to teach children how special they are for just being alive and being who they were born to be which is just, "themselves." We need to empower our children to do and become their best. If we build their confidence that they can do and become anything their heart desires, they really will feel they can do anything and ultimately will. We need to help them discover their creative spirit, to write, draw, and paint, play an instrument or excel in their favorite sport. They are our future leaders in this world and we need to nurture their abilities so the future will become a better one then perhaps times past and we their teachers need to lovingly teach them."

"As the old saying transcends to us, people enter our lives for, 'a reason, a season or a lifetime.' We never know at first why and to what extent these people will enter our lives to help us grow and mature in ways we didn't know we could or would, but they do. Only time will tell us for which reason, season or the length of our lifetime they will be there for us, but each relationship can bring us and tell us things we need to know about ourselves that we were not ready to know and accept that we may be ready for now."

"Become global friendly. We can do this by respecting the earth and if we want the earth to exist for generations to come, then we have to be the ones to make sure we recycle, clean our surroundings and give back to the world in healthy loving ways for our future families and future generations to appreciate and enjoy."

"We should never have to pay for friendship. The true friends in our lives should be people who want to like us for ourselves, not because we buy them presents or offer them something which haven't any bearing on them liking us. People will like us or not like us for being just ourselves so we should not look for things to offer people to be our friends except our time, our caring, our love and just 'our everlasting friendship.'"

"When we are unsure about some situation or a friend we know who hasn't called us back or written to us or just hasn't been attentive to the relationship that we have with them, until we know for sure just have faith and believe that all will turn out okay. Sometimes things aren't what they appear to be and the stories in our head can get carried away, so until we know for sure always try to believe the best, instead of the worst. Our friends have their own lives too and sometimes theirs can be so chaotic, that certain things such as a good friendship that was in the forefront may now be on the backburner and we may think it is us but not always, but I believe that some lives go in different directions too. What was important to us one day may not be the next. This goes for relationships with our family members, friends or anyone we may know. So, always give them benefit of the doubt until we know for sure."

"Some of our friendships will be casual, some friends will get together each week, and some friendships will be universal and lifelong. We may not see family and friends for a long time, or see or hear from them but when there is a life issue such as sickness, death of a loved one or something as significant we can be sure others will rise to the occasion and be there as if they had never left."

"Build a friendship with, 'a special needs person,' so they feel as IMPORTANT as everyone else. With this special act, all involved feel GREAT rightly so. We should never do so out of pity (because they don't need or want it), but only out of FRIENDSHIP. We need to treat all people in the same way we would want them to treat us and that is with respect, kindness and love."

Chapter 2:

HAPPINESS, GRATITUDE AND APPRECIATION

In my journey through life I have experienced the blessings of happiness, gratitude and appreciation. These are three concepts that when I have embraced them they have changed my life and turned me into the man I have become and whom I look forward to becoming still. I feel in my heart that these three concepts are some of the beginning stages we need to start out with in order to benefit from the fruits of having a most fulfilling life.

I feel happiness begins when we genuinely feel we are grateful and appreciative for all we have in this world. The joyous feeling of happiness, gratitude and appreciation should be what motivates us to begin each day, continue throughout the day and then end each day. The world as a whole can and is filled with sadness, war, destruction and pain. Everyday we may have tough challenges that take us into the dark regions where nothing is positive. These places are ones we do not want to live in and set up shop and yet from time to time we find ourselves surrounded in them. In order for us to leave those darkened places, we need to find the light. We need to cleanse our minds as well as our bodies of the negativity and darkness that can pull us down so far we cannot see straight or think coherently.

The light I believe can and will be found by seeking and acknowledging all the blessings we have that are here today and sadly gone tomorrow. We need to be actively sincere in thankfulness for our blessings and in doing so happiness, gratitude and appreciation will then be in the forefront of our minds and daily attitudes.

We should begin each day as I do with a prayer of thanks for all the blessings bestowed upon me by God and His angels above and for this beautiful new day of life. Each day just like a rainbow after the rains can be a rebirth, a new beginning, and a chance to begin again. Whatever mistakes we have made yesterday or way back in our past, today is a new day to rectify them.

We can change whatever we thought we did wrong or could have made better and have this day to do just that. Each of our days is a blessing that we should be aware of and treat as such.

If each of us thought this way in good and in hard times, we would feel more grateful for our life and life in general. Our lives would be healthier and happier and we would be more grateful for all that has been bestowed upon us. We are here to make this world shine for the better and when we know and act as if we are blessed and grateful it will show in all that we do and work on to accomplish. Of course, we all want more good times and less bad times, but being grateful and happy inside will help to diminish any pain that the hard times can surely bring to us.

Each of us with so little effort can find what is wrong within our lives and in those lives in the world that live outside our front door and around the globe. It is so easy to find people whose daily lives include heartache and pain, with what seems as if there is no way out. The world outside our door can be a scary place; and it is. Yet, sometimes we are going through a crisis in our lives and we feel it in our bones from head to toe. In those times, it can be very difficult to be grateful when sadness and pain fill our hearts. We all go through this including myself.

Instead, what I believe we must do is happily search for in our lives what is good and what we can change to make better. We can create this with just the feeling of wanting to and doing so. I have worked on and finished three "thank you and gratitude journals," in three years worth of time. For this I give thanks to Sarah Ban Breathnach and Oprah Winfrey. They inspired me to do this and what I have received is a life filled with abundance. Each day I would write five things I am grateful for in just that one day alone. If we keep our heads and hearts open each day we will discover so many new things to appreciate and to be grateful for. Sometimes even after a bad day of work it may have been difficult to find five, in this case I would choose things that I am universally thankful for. Even sometimes after a horrible day at work, I would write, "I am happy to have a job and a paycheck." I wrote this to remind me of how lucky I was and am, because so many do not have a job or a paycheck.

I would include those and realize that my life is a blessing and I have so much to be grateful for and that my cup no matter what, is ALWAYS half full and is surely OVERFLOWING.

We need to be a society that is thankful, grateful and appreciative for "all," that we have. Some people I meet say that "things could always be worse." This is so true, and there are others who say "it could be better." What I would say to these statements is this, "We have to be the ones who make it better." It will not happen on its own, for how can it be when we are not conscious of the things to be grateful for, to make our lives better. We have to be pro-active to get the results we want. As we all know there are good times and bad times for all of us, but knowing that it is our responsibility to do the best we can and make so much good outweigh any bad that could mess up our lives.

I have heard it said that we must be "happy," first; and only then will our circumstances change. Because if we just sit and wait for our "circumstances," to change first then we will never be happy. Even if we pretend first we are happy and then look for the blessings that we have been bestowed with we will in time feel good, grateful and happy.

As I live and work my life to create the jewels of happiness, gratitude and appreciation, I know it is a daily job of mine to believe that these ideas can become my reality. The loving reality of waking up each day and blessing the day by saying thank you dear God for my family, friends, and my writing ability; Thank you dear God for the ability to help others less fortunate than I; Thank you dear God for food and water, as well as a roof over my head and a job and paycheck to pay for them. These are some of the greatest blessings we can ever ask for and we should be reminded of them all the time.

We have so much more than so many people living around the world from far away and from people who live probably next door to us. If we have a good decent roof over our heads and fresh food in our refrigerator, a good job that is paying us enough to have that roof over our heads and food in our refrigerators then we are so blessed. There are many people whose quality of living is below poverty lines that it is sad and disheartening when our country is so rich. When people in this world have so little and we have so much and we pretend or close our eyes to what we do have and what others lack we are not being appreciative to what we have.

We are just being selfish. But if we wake up each day and be thankful for the fact that we did "just wake up," and look at our surroundings and who we have in our lives and what we stand for as a person this is the best way to begin to start to feel happy, grateful and appreciative for our gifts in life.

If we are to be happy in our lifetime, we have to not want or need so much. We need to be satisfied with what we have and not feel that we are not like everyone else who has to have the latest technical gadget to be happy. We all lived with none of these technical gadgets for most of time. All this is new and as time goes on the world will make us think that we need all of what we truly do not need.

What we truly "need," is just to be thankful for just being alive and having some of the nice things that life can offer, even when some of what life can give us is undesirable. We have been blessed with "the gift of life," and being thankful for this is a wonderful beginning and it is then our chance to take the next steps and make it the best life we can possibly make. With this we can have a life of happiness, be grateful and have appreciation for all that matters and what we will discover is that we have found "true sincere," happiness. I truly want it for everyone.

"A great way to start the day I have found is to say 'Thank You, Dear God' for the gift of my life,' and then I do my best to use it and live it well. We've been blessed with a new day to begin again and fix what might not have worked yesterday. Things may have gone wrong the day before and may not have been fixed by the day's end, so by the following day we have a chance to repair any damage and start from a better place and perspective."

"Always be grateful and thankful for the gifts that each day can bring to each and every one of us. Each day is a chance to forgive others and create better more fulfilling friendships and relationships with all people on this earth."

"We need to be thankful and appreciative of the people in our lives, and the things that we have at this very moment and not seek to always need more. We have so much more than many people around the world. Some people have nothing and are desperate for food, while we are living high on the hog. So always say 'thank you,' and always be 'appreciative,' and 'always give back to the universe and its people.' "

"Be thankful by saying 'Thank you Dear God' for the 'small things,' in life as well as the 'big things.' Those small things that we just take for granted sometimes are the very things that seem to just get us through the day when nothing else can and we need to acknowledge them with thanks."

"The basic expressions of our language which include 'Please and Thank you' need to be used more often than not in this world to each other; otherwise we can sound ungrateful for so much that we need to be appreciative of."

'Be thankful for the gift of sight, there are many people who do not have this beautiful gift to actually see a rainbow after a rainstorm, or a smile on someone's face. Be thankful for the gift of hearing, some do not know this gift to hear the beautiful sounds of a song and their instruments, or the beautiful sound of a speaking voice reading Shakespeare as it transcends thru the air. Be thankful for the food we are given and the fresh water we have, because there are people around the world who have no food and their water is tainted. Always give thanks for these things and never take them for granted because when we are blessed and have the good in this world, know that it could have been and still might be turned around where we will miss those things that we should have held so dearly."

"Send and give hope, guidance, love, compassion and your miracles to other people in need. When we transcend this gracious act to others it gets returned to us in wonderful and magical ways."

"It is important that we become generous people. Giving to others makes us feel good as well as we hope to the receiver. Being generous doesn't mean we have to be rich and give money all the time since most of us aren't rich. Giving of our time and energy is a very important part of generosity. We give to others and by doing so the universe is very grateful for our giving nature and then it sends it back to us when we need the help."

"If we count our blessings daily and even write them down in a 'thank you journal,' we will see in a tangible way how truly lucky we are. Learn to become gracious, thankful and loving people and we will feel blessed with all that we have and can give to others."

"Sometimes we do not realize just how truly lucky we are in this world. No matter at what age problems can and do arise that can threaten our mortal existence. As children or adults we can come down with diseases that could take away precious years ahead of us. Some people are born in parts of the world that wars live constantly and their lives could end at any moment. Some people are born into families that force them to live as they do sometimes against their will or the consequences could be harmful and deadly. Some of us could come from a life filled with constant struggle day in and day out with no relief in sight. So I believe when our life doesn't have these type struggles per say, we can look at our lives and know that yes we do have good days and bad ones, but just maybe our life isn't as bad as sometimes it "appears" to be. It could always be worse and we can always make it better. If we examine what is on our plate compared to what others have or what could be on ours we would consciously be thankful. We would thank our Creator and pray for others who have less on their plate. We would also pray that we should all live and be happy."

"It is important to be appreciated for what we do at home or at the office or wherever we do our jobs. To go day in and day out to our place of work whether at home or in the workforce with no incentive that by which a few kind words could help the morale of workers, then not as much work would be accomplished. Even though we may know we are doing good productive work it is always nice to hear it from our bosses or the people we care for. Just to hear the words that all the effort we put in to our work is appreciated makes for a healthier person and work and home environment."

"Never feel the need to always to be right, because you will never be happy. Feeling the need to be right all the time affords us nothing. There is just no happy ending in this. It is okay to know we are right sometimes when it surely makes sense. Then there are other times when just letting it go will make for a healthy mind and spirit. 'Let it go,' should be the motto, just "Let it go."

"Always bless the rains for they bring water to help the trees, plants and flowers grow. The rains also give nourishment to the people, animals and wildlife of the earth as well as to the environment."

"Fill your life with laughter. Because, yes it is the best medicine we have for sadness, pain and depression."

"I once heard this said so eloquently about materialism from the 1970's CBS children's show 'Shazam," which I paraphrased 'Nothing we collect in our lifetime truly belongs to us…we only borrow them while we are here.' This pertains, to people, animals, nature or all things we collect and think we own once in our possession. Once we learn that concept that 'it all stays here,' and nothing comes with us we begin to respect and cherish life more deeply and profoundly. I hope you will cherish your life and those around you more deeply and profoundly."

Chapter 3

A WORLD WITH MORE KINDNESS AND COMPASSION

I feel that it is so vitally important that we restore our world's beauty. I feel if enough of us work toward that, we can do that. How you might ask? By constantly showing and giving to all others our kindness and compassion whether we know them or do not; whether they can give us everything or cannot give us anything, still express your kindness and compassion to everyone and all living things. Whether we realize it or not we are truly one spirit living and moving in separate bodies. When we express kindness to others; when we show caring and compassion for other human beings we are showing it to ourselves as well and we all benefit. What a great blessing this gift is!!!

I see a world that I know I want to change for the better. I see a world with so many wars going on and people fighting that sometimes our hearts and souls get misplaced. We need to try and dig out of the rubble and aftermath and then we need to replace what was 'misplaced,' and that is our "kindness and compassion," for one another as human beings that walk this planet individually and collectively.

The Dalai Lama has been quoted as saying, "My religion is very simple. My religion is kindness," and this is one that we should all join, no matter what we're born into or make of our own choosing, "kindness," should be our way of life. In all areas of my life and world, I want to project on to others that I want the best for them as I would want for anyone. I do so by showing others kindness in our interactions. Any behavior that goes against kindness is not the way for us to be acting toward one another. We feel so good inside when we are giving in our nature of being respectful to another person and doing kind things for them and it is nice to see the appreciation others show back to us when we have been kind to them and vice versa.

By being giving in our nature and considerate of others we set up the universe to treat us the same way in the people we meet and greet, and interact with. I know in my own life how important it is to do that and by my example, I hope I can give others a desire to do that in their own lives. The act of compassion is in its most purist form "a most loving act," that we can give others in this world as well as to ourselves.

The definition of "compassion," from Dictionary.com is: "a feeling of deep sympathy and sorrow for another who is stricken by misfortune, accompanied by a strong desire to alleviate the suffering." The first part of the meaning: "a feeling of deep sympathy and sorrow for another who is stricken by misfortune," I know for me that from the deepest core of my soul when someone I know or do not know is feeling a deep sense of loss and sorrow how could I not become affected by it, it being their pain and sadness. No matter what someone is going through, a sense of loss from the death of a loved one, job, their home, from a flood, tornado or an earthquake, as we've seen in Haiti in January 2010, Hurricane Katrina in 2005, or our own recent Hurricane Sandy in 2012, so many lives are affected, and if not now someday I or someone I love could be experiencing a loss as great as theirs or worse. Therefore, I know and feel it is natural for me to feel their suffering and loss. What if I was in their situation, I know I would want others to be there for me, show compassion from what I have been experiencing, and help me.

The second part of the Dictionary.com meaning of compassion is: "accompanied by a strong desire to alleviate the suffering." We I hope can all agree that we would want to take away someone's pain and hurt. We would all want to alleviate any and all suffering they might be going through. Being there for someone is so important when the chips are down, their life has taken the turn for the worst, or they are experiencing the sad loss of their loved one or friend. We all have the strong desire to replace any pain and sadness with love, light, hope and a bright future for the person or persons feeling the pain. Perhaps a friend or someone you love or even a co-worker or stranger came down with a disease or has been in a car accident, by expressing our hope and compassion for someone it sends something extraordinary out into the universe and hopefully to that person that all is not lost and hope is there and will continue to be there.

When I see someone who is in pain, walking with a cane, walker or an elderly person, I know they have experienced something that can make them need the assistance of another person, and when I see this and know this just by looking at them do I know that both kindness and compassion is the greatest gift I can offer them and will do so lovingly. I feel we should all feel this way and act in this way.

What a wonderful world this would be if we poured love into it and less of everything else. If we took kindness and compassion and spread it across the universe to all the people that walk the planet, how wonderful that would be. If each person could stop thinking about themselves, power, prestige, wanting to know the "right," people and instead used that powerful energy to just send love to each other. If we could show a lot more kindness, show a lot more compassion and see how it would grow just like a flower in a garden how brighter and more beautiful would this planet be. To be able to stop racist and hateful behavior and just reversed it toward more loving behavior this world would become a unified world instead of a separate world.

    We have a world filled with so many opposites such as democrats, republicans, gay, straight, right, wrong. Why can we not become a world of the same things or be on the same side. When 9/11 happened it showed that we could put all our differences aside and joined together to help each other and what this did was show how great we can truly be when we arise to the occasion and step up to the plate. What we did is come together. What we did is put aside all things that did not matter and show what did matter. We brought our compassion to a horrific situation and brought our kindness to people we never met before. We might have made friends that would last a lifetime from this or just helped others because it was the "right thing," to do and what we should all be doing all the time.

    We should be showing respect to the elderly and the sickly. These people who we see as elderly and or sickly can be us someday because we are just as human as they are and we are no different than they are. As we get older our motor skills may slow us down and we might not have the energy that we once had so we tend to not run or move as quickly as we did in our younger days.

Sometimes a disease or something hits us and we need a cane, a wheel chair or an accident put us in a place that we never thought about before and now we do and we must face the present and the future with our present circumstances. By being kind to others and showing compassion for the plight of others, we are setting up the universe that the compassion and kindness we gave to others will surely be returned to us "when and if," we find ourselves in situations that we had wished had never happened. But we do not just want to pretend to be tolerable or even nice to the sick and or elderly. They do not want our pity, but respect for someone else's pain feels right and is the right thing to do. Moreover, we may make them feel better and give them encouragement when we show the basic of human emotions: kindness and compassion.

The act and the feelings that kindness transcends shows people that there are others out there that care about us and we about them. We are a world filled with human beings with human emotions and when there is a world filled with a lack of love, friendship, kindness and compassion, we just can lose our way and ability to do great things in this world. With the building blocks of kindness and compassion, we feel so great inside that it can inspire us to be the best we can possibly be. There are so many people in this world that would do anything to destroy the hope in others and to gain power and prestige and couldn't careless about others. They think only of themselves, their needs and what they can gain from what others can give them, and helping others and showing kindness to others is not in their life's repertoire of living. This I believe is so sad because this world would be and can be and I believe still is a beautiful loving world where kindness and compassion still lives and breathes as a main factor of life, even though there is death, destruction, and evil in the world.

    We all have a choice to bless others with our kindness and compassion or not, but then look at your life and see what's going well and what's not and look for the reasons and then change them. Perhaps the lack in your life is because you are not giving more kindness and compassion to others. Start now and see how your life will change in miraculous ways.

    What happens when we turn on the news each day? We see so much bad news either in the lives of others or the economy. People have lost their homes and jobs, in other parts of the globe or even in our own country, we have earthquakes, floods, murder and wars going on. Where is the good news, where are the stories of you and me where we are making a difference and trying to make more, "good news," in the world override that, "bad news," that we hear about constantly. We need to put more kindness and compassion into this world and spread happiness and love and what I believe comes out and back is a better world, a more loving world and a world with lives that want to make a difference and a contribution to society. Maybe then when more kindness and compassion over rule the world, less wars and evil will want to live and breathe in the world. However, it is up to you and me to be the bringers of kindness and compassion back into this world and maybe then a more loving world this world would be.

"Be a person who expresses love, friendship and kindness to others, and what you find is it gets returned back to you in ways that are far more incredible than you could ever have imagined."

"When getting to know people ask them about their personal side such as, "how is your family?' 'Where do you originate from?' etc. It shows them you care about them and their life circumstances. We appreciate it when we are asked about our lives and it would be nice if we did so in kind."

"If someone's family member is not feeling well, the next time you see them ask them, "How are you doing? I hope your feeling better. I was thinking about you." Make a phone call; write an e-mail; do whatever feels right to see if that person is feeling well again. We really do appreciate it when people show concern for us and even our loved ones especially when we do not expect it."

"When we pass someone with a disability or an elderly person with a walker, or visibly not filled with energy or a healthy spirit, a gracious thing would be is to say a prayer for them, smile at them and wish them well. That person could be US one day and we would want good wishes and prayers tossed in our direction that our pain that we may experience be eased and healed sooner rather than later."

"If you pass someone day after day sitting outside their front door such as an elderly person; SMILE and say HELLO. Two powerful acts of kindness sends a powerful message to the other person that says someone cares enough to acknowledge their existence especially later in life as well as any part of life. Each day while walking to work I would notice this elderly woman in her wheel chair along with her home attendant and after seeing them day after day I would just smile and say, "hello," as I passed them. People want to know that at any age they matter to others. Just because they are not in some 'limelight,' or 'the center of attention,' all people need to feel they are still viable in the world. Saying hello to this woman may have brightened her day and it did mine as well. This is kindness and compassion at work in the world and yes this can change our planet."

"Even though I believe no one really owes us anything in this life, (this statement meaning that there are some people that '**expect**,' things from others and if they 'don't get what they **demand**,' then how dare the other person.) This type of thinking will get us nowhere. But with that being said, I do believe each of us owes each other '**everything**,' as fellow human beings on this planet. We all need to get along, respect each other and build together the greatest and brightest that humanity can become and kindness and compassion I know will surely get us there."

"When we do kindnesses for each other it is because it is 'the right thing,' and the 'nice thing,' to do, but we should not expect people all the time to do great things for us, when we give nothing in return such as a simple 'thank you,' or 'a show of gratitude.' It is just as important to give to others as well as to receive and when we recognize this fact and put it into action we will find that both sides are happier people. Then both sides continue giving and paying it forward and then it makes for a healthier universe of people."

"When we ask someone for a favor and they do this kindness for us, we must not in that realm of being shown this favor or kindness, tell or ask the person doing this kindness for us 'can you also do this for me and can you be quick about it.' I know working in a doctor's office and patients come in without an appointment and we are happy to help them as long as they are willing to wait. Then they ask for another favor and they want us to hurry up. I feel we should be thankful someone is doing a kindness for us and let it be. Do not take advantage of the other person or else the kindnesses may stop. Whether it is in the doctor's office, waiting at the grocery line or through friendship we should not 'abuse,' those kindnesses. We will one day soon realize when there is no more kindness coming in our direction from others hopefully we will realize why and then learn from that and become better people, then one day the acts of new kindnesses from others may begin again and that is always a blessing."

"Do something wonderful for another human being. Just let them know someone cares about them. Buy them lunch, or a cup of coffee, or pay for their bus fare. With this simple act of kindness, all involved feel profoundly blessed to be alive and that we do matter to others. Showing others they truly matter is the greatest gift we can give others as well as to ourselves."

"When someone is sick or in pain, pray for them that they heal quickly. Pray to God, His loving angels, the universe and the powers that be, that the person you are praying for does heal quickly, this holy instant. This, another holy loving act of compassion toward another human being is what will bring us closer together, which should be humanities goal."

"Giving a hug or receiving a hug can be the greatest of healing medicines on this planet. We all need hugs and it feels just as great for the giver as it is for the receiver. Give one to family members, friends, co-workers and even a stranger if they need one. You will make someone's day and is this not our life's purpose, making someone feel wanted and loved and that they matter?."

Chapter 4

CARING ABOUT OTHER PEOPLE AND OURSELVES

Being caring individuals to ourselves and other people should be a most fervent goal in our lives. It makes so much sense. If we care about others both we and the other person or persons feel so loved inside and appreciated that a change in our world has taken place in a direction all will want to follow. A road or path that says I matter, you matter, we all matter to one another. Can life be better than that? Once the gift of caring about other people and ourselves has taken flight in the world we make better choices in our lives and in that we become better people. The world can only benefit thereby in blessings and gifts and love for one another.

It is important to be a giver in this world, a person who wants the best for others and because of that will show their caring side in full awareness that others will appreciate that side and allow their caring nature to also come out in full bloom.

With that loving thought and picture that we must care about others, I believe though in my own experience that we always must be caring and thoughtful of ourselves first. How could we ever take care of other people and be concerned for their welfare and the help they would need when we ourselves may at times be running on empty. I know when I was going through depression and anxiety, the world outside to me was a place where I could not be of help, because I was going through such emotional pain. How could I give to others when I could not give to myself?

Yes there are times when mental and/or physical pain can put us in a place that it is just too hard to be there for other people and to help them. It is a struggle and we must find ways to cope and deal and come to a place where we can nurture ourselves, find peace in our pain so we can reawaken to a wonderful place that we felt was closed off to us during our asleep state. Once reawakened we can return to the wonderful things life has to offer us and we can then start helping others and return to that caring nature all of us deserve to experience as both the giver and the receiver.

It is never ever selfish to want to care, nurture and become loving to ourselves; to make sure we are mentally and physically well, eating better, exercising, going to the doctor routinely, getting plenty of sleep and doing fun things to take away the blahs from a bad day. This is how I have run my life. Is it selfish? I believe it is only selfish when we only care about ourselves and not for anyone else. When we use the words, "me, my and I," all the time and not words such as "you, us and we," we become selfish people and it is what we put out into the universe and what we put out comes back to us accordingly. Therefore, if we are showing others that we only care about ourselves then selfish people come into our lives, which extend into our relationships at home and at work, and at any place we spend time. We attract what we give out and when we are thinking about ourselves, our needs, and what we can get with little or no concern for others our lives are not going to be the best that it can be. Taking time for ourselves to regroup is important and once this is complete we should do what we can for others in our families, our friendships, our relationships at work and in our communities.

The questions should always be: "How can I make this person's life better?" How can I help other people young, elderly and everyone in between? At every age we go through something. We either have life struggles, including sickness, illness, life altering diseases and we all need help at different times in our lives. We as a society, nation and planet need to be there for each other to provide this help.

We also experience the beauty of life such as birthdays, anniversaries, graduations, and special occasions. We have different religions, spiritual practices all which make this world a much more beautiful place, especially when we extend it with LOVE. The coming together and celebration of life and all the beautiful things it has to offer is each of our blessings. Each religion, each culture and sect of society have their own joyous occasions and the world has universal times that we all celebrate and remember the past, accept and enjoy the now and look forward to a brighter and better tomorrow if we are blessed to arrive there safely, which I hope and pray we all do.

      When the question is asked, "why should we care about other people besides ourselves?" The answer should always be, 'because the soul of humanity's existence wins when we show caring and concern for our human family." When we show the best of our humanity, all of the planet and its people benefit. When we give the gift of caring to each other; a gift that is already in us to give innately we will feel blessed with peace and contentment, the cost of which is so small and the price and rewards are beyond what the mind can comprehend. Is this not the way we were meant to spend our lives, giving the best of ourselves to others? When we do this it goes out into the universe and comes back to us and we again send it back out to all the people who need our caring and our help, our love and our time. I know how wonderful inside and out I feel when I have donated to a charity, or participated in a charity walk, or helped random people that have come into my life. I know the best part of me shines and in doing so the universe will shine back on me and in my life as well.

    I want to know that my time has been spent on this earth caring about other people and making a difference in their lives. If I take care of myself, I can come to the aid of others and make the lives of others feel important. We all need to feel important and make others feel that way too. When we do this, a better life, planet and world will exist and humanity will start to exist in complete bliss. With humanity in complete bliss, maybe there will be new beginnings for us to experience less war and destruction, famine and disease. Maybe if we all come together as one complete spirit of humanity from different cultures, religions and diverse places we can become one group that just comes together and makes things easier for one another instead of more difficult. We must extend our love and caring for all humanity, the earth, the environment and animals. I look forward for us coming together and becoming one. Yes a planet of people who loves and cares for one another. Let that gift of caring for other people and ourselves begin, today, right now. I care about you and hope you feel the same about me and all of God's children.

"First be caring and loving to yourself and then when you do, you can be caring, more loving and there for others in this world. How can we ever expect to help others when we haven't even taken care of ourselves first? Once you have taken care of yourself, you should then extend that to others and help our world change for the better. Thank you."

"Always be who you are and what you are (sans any negative or unloving qualities). Never let others make you feel anything less than what or who you were born to be. No race, creed, color or sexual orientation should be put down, ridiculed or made to feel they are any less worthy than anyone else. Show caring, love and respect to all of God's children. If we do, then the world has begun to become a more beautiful one for all of us to share in."

"If we can take care of our own needs first, then we will be able to help others more easily, because then we will be in better spirits then a more energized light will emerge fully to be a caring spirit that walks our world that cares for one another."

"As much as all of us want to be in a relationship with another person, we should first be in a relationship with ourselves. Become happy living in our own skin, knowing our likes and dislikes, making a successful life for ourselves and ONLY be in a relationship when we want to share things with others. We need to do our own inner work to ensure our mind, body and spirit are aligned with love. Then we can bring someone else into our life to share life's joys with us. We want and need love, friendship, and a caring companionship. Each coming to the relationship and bringing different things that the other person might lack and teaching the other which will make them one. We don't want a relationship so we can feel like a whole person. We need to be a whole person before entering into a relationship. We just want to join two people of loving souls and spirits into oneness. These loving souls will share good times, but also be there when the chips are down and loss may enter another's life and be there to comfort them. This is what we all want for our lives and should be blessed enough to attain it. Then the magic of two souls joining together will be one of reverence and be the example for others to have in their life."

Chapter 5

LEARNING, GROWING, AND KNOWING

I have always felt good about myself when I was learning something or wanted to learn something that would make me become smarter, well-read or would grow as a person. When I was growing up perhaps I didn't appreciate school as I would now and learning by reading and listening to others is something I treasure now more than ever. I read books and listen to audio CDS and radio shows on topics of interest that would help me grow from an average person to a more profound one. The idea of learning, then growing, and knowing is an idea I want to see come to fruition for myself and I would love the concept to grow in others.

When I hear that there are adults in this world who cannot read and write, this saddens me so. Because of this fact back in 1998, I was lucky enough to volunteer my time with the "Brooklyn Public Library Adult Literacy Program" and teach adults to read and write. I had about five people in my group. Two of them stayed for many weeks and three of them stayed my entire run. I had a sweet African American woman , and two lovely

Muslim women also very sweet and I enjoyed teaching them all that I could. These women were there because they wanted to improve themselves. They wanted to become better people and to do this they had to learn how to read and to write. I believe they learned that this world can be closed off to us if we do not know the basics such as reading and writing.

The "Library Learning Center," which was a free opportunity was the place for them to be and a place that I needed to be that way I could be of service to them. I set up lessons from the criteria of what the learning center set forth. I hope in the end they came away with a good start to learning and a chance to start them on the right road. When I had to leave and start a new job they gave me a cake and a nice cup "Worlds Best Teacher," which I still have to this day. It's very nice that they thought I was able to help them and I sincerely hope I did. I hope sixteen years later they are doing well and reading and writing fluently.

If we are lucky we have had our parents to help us learn along with mentors, teachers and friends as well as religious and spiritual leaders. They are the first to take our not knowing and mold it into something that brings us toward knowledge. We come from not knowing and as in Zen Buddhism we have what is called "a beginners mind." It's like holding out an empty rice bowl to God. If it is filled up we cannot fill it up further with deeper understanding and growth. But if we empty our rice bowl we will have more room for knowledge and growth. When we were children we always had the awe of wonderment, not knowing and asking questions to learn, grow and understand what we had not before. This is something that we should always have and yet we become adults and we think that we "know it all," and "have it all," figured out. We need to have that childlike mentality of always asking more questions and not thinking that we go into a situation knowing all. Because then we cannot learn more. Our minds are closed to learning and knowing more than we could learn had we kept it open to receiving.

    Our parents teach us in the home how to act and take care of ourselves and how to function in the world. Our teachers in school teach us the basics of reading, writing and general math. We learn about social studies and geography and all the necessary information to lead us into adulthood. Our religious and spiritual leaders will help us to gain inner strength and help us learn the power of prayer and our belief in God, and the universe and how to live a more loving, holy and spiritual existence.

    These are just some of the first teachers in our

lives to help us in learning, growing and knowing what we should to become the best people we are destined to become and hope to become.

The fact that we are given the gift to learn, comprehend and attain knowledge is such a precious gift that we sometimes take it for granted. We accept the fact that we know what we know and that there is no other reason to further grow and attain more fruitful knowledge. We stop at a certain point and that's it. Learning, growing and knowing are the first steps but there is always room and until we leave this world, we should always be learning something. Thank God for that ability to be able to learn something new and hopefully valuable. As we get older our values change and the need to learn different things takes form. What I learned growing up was important at that stage and would eventually lead me to the place I am now; a mature forty-something year old man who wants to digest more and more valuable information on different topics and different subjects. I want to learn about spirituality and different religions that exist in the world. I want to learn about the differences in people as well as the things that unite us as a people. I enjoy learning about how to make our lives better. I want to do it for myself as well as to teach others.

It has always been my passion reading books

because books have been the place where knowledge lives and breathes. I have my house filled with books. Many of the books I have read and many I have not read as of yet and though I just love having them in my home and around me. I bring them with me on the bus or anywhere I have to go to keep me company. I love going to the library and bookstores. Books have always been the staple in my life and hope it will always be.

    I think that once we have gained knowledge and we did our learning and growing it is time to become the teacher and to teach others. To teach others shows us that we have learned many things as we were supposed to and now it is time to pass that along to others. Whether it be the children, adults who cannot read and write, the elderly or anyone who wants to learn and wants us to be there to teach them, we should be there for them to give them whatever knowledge we have attained that might do them well in this world. Some of the elderly who obviously were here before we were could teach us many things as well and we should always be open to it and revere and respect our elders for the fact that they were here before us and because of what they could teach us.

    Unfortunately, there can be people from any age who keep their minds closed and will not learn a thing and want to become possessed by their egos and do not want to become people who grow and mature by learning the important things in life. Learning important things and values such as how to be "a kind and caring person," or "the importance of doing things for others," and not just learn what they could do for themselves, how rich or how materialistic their lives could be and are. Some think they can go to school, graduate from college having learned a trade or academia and go out into the world having the wonderful opportunity to become rich but sadly never care if the person next to them lives or dies.

To me learning, growing, and knowing is a stepping stone to becoming the best we can be for at first ourselves and then for all the people in our lives and in the lives of whom we meet. These are the people in our lives and in this world that will bring us up and lift us forward.

The early teachers in our lives were there for their job of teaching us and now it is up to us to do the same for others and future generations. I believe that we are on this earth to learn and then to teach and make this world so much better than perhaps we've seen in the past. It is up to you and me to cultivate the world with not just knowledge but compassion, kindness and then watch it lead toward wisdom. I know in my life these are the steps I must take to ensure I pass on the beliefs that led the way for me. This life is a journey and it is the responsibility for each of us to help others lead the way in the best way they see fit. Some of the beliefs may differ but in the end we all want and deserve the same things; divine health, happiness, joy and peace and a willingness to learn and grow, which leads to knowing and then to teaching others. When we are able to teach others; the younger crowd who are moving into the place we just moved out of and the cycle of life moves forward and wisdom is pouring forth I believe we know we have kept life's learning process moving in a healthy direction. If we all put our faith in learning and we become knowledgeable we can change and grow into better living souls who live upon this earth and teach others. Is this not what life is for and is it not our responsibility to make sure it happens, so we can say we lived our lives well by learning, growing and then teaching others? Let us obtain the gift of learning and then extend the gift of our knowledge to that of teaching others. Here's to an awakened world.

"One of the greatest tools we have in this world are our teachers and our mentors. They can teach and guide us and make us better people reaching for our highest selves. Some of our best teachers and mentors are our parents, family members and friends, teachers at school, and religious or spiritual leaders. We can read books, listen to great singers and read the uplifting words of great writers. If we choose to ask for help, we just may be able to get the best help and advice we could ever imagine and live our best days."

"Become a knowledgeable person on any topic that embraces your soul. If we listen and learn we will understand and what will graciously follow is that we will become enlightened individuals who teach others to become awakened as well."

"Become a powerful leader in something that you feel you can lead in. Becoming a leader in something that doesn't have your soul will not carry you through or move the cause along. Believe in something and leadership will follow and then others will join you on those endeavors."

"Forgiveness takes work. It is not always easy when so many feelings are stirred and our egos get involved. In the book "A Course in Miracles," that I read and do the workbook exercises, forgiveness is a major part of the ideas and we must learn to forgive others in order that we may be happy ourselves. We all want to be happy and we should not want to be disingenuous to others and we should be in a forgiving nature. Once the smoke clears, just let whatever was so important at the time be released and let forgiveness win out. We need not hold grievances or grudges. This does not mean that we are a doormat with anyone, or they are not responsible for their actions, but just letting the anger be released and moving on and we do this by genuinely letting the anger and hurt dissipate, because in time it won't be that important. This concept was something I had to learn and apply in my life. I had to learn not to hold grudges and not to hold grievances toward others. Not speaking to someone that either I lived with or worked with or a friend because I thought they may have done me wrong or something was said in anger and I held on to it like a vice. We need to let it go, and realize that we are much freer when our hearts are not so heavy."

"Sometimes we will meet wonderful people during different times in our lives, and even though the relationship may not be long lasting, they do have special meaning for us and may last in our memory and emotional lifetime. This will carry us along our journey and may even help us during a rough time. So always be willing to look at all relationships with something to teach us."

"There are some people who "just don't get it." They choose to see things one way, their way, the only way and nothing can penetrate them to a more enlightened way of thinking. This is very sad because seeing things only one way with no dimensions lessens us from growing and maturing. Other people cannot and should not embrace the negativity these people bring to the table. Because in actuality they bring nothing to the table except "it's their way or the highway," mentality, and this serves no one, it only draws us away from these kinds of people."

"When we feel good about ourselves, losing sometimes is okay. We cannot always win and that should be OKAY. If we feel good inside about ourselves, losing sometimes "does not and should not matter." Hey sometimes we might win and feel great, but knowing that we always cannot win, we should also continue to feel great and know that next time will be better. JUST ALWAYS DO YOUR BEST. This should be ENOUGH."

"Always 'ADMIRE,' people, never 'ENVY,' them. We should admire people that have some wonderful qualities and attributes that they bring to the forefront that we may appreciate and may want to emulate. This is wonderful. But we should never 'envy,' someone else which says "I wish I wasn't who I am and wish I was someone else with attributes, which may not even fit me." Be who you are and do not try to become something your not. People will appreciate us for who we are and what we can bring to the table. Where someone is great at computers, someone else may be great with a paintbrush or numbers, business or science. So 'admire,' people and try to learn how to do something which emulates your own talents, and don't 'envy,' someone and wish you had their gifts. Each of us has our own gifts and we need to make them work and shine for the benefit of all."

"Sometimes we look at other people and they are at a younger age then us and seemed to have accomplished so much at such an early age, while we seem to either have not accomplished so much or have accomplished some things but at long intervals or are 'late bloomers.' We should never feel sad or bitter at this. Each person is different, our goals or the way we do things may be different, but each life accomplishes things in its own time, and we should never feel any less important than those who accomplish things quicker or at an age where others look with amazement. We are all worthy people and each of us grows, matures and accomplishes at a different pace. So we should never judge our lives at any point as not having accomplished so much at any given time. It is over the course of someone's life and looking back that we will have accomplished so much, each at a different pace and when the time for us is right. A fine wine is not ready before its time and neither can we be. Treasure what you have done and just prepare for what you will do when the time is right."

Chapter 6

IF WE LIVE OUR LIVES WITH INTEGRITY OUR LIVES WILL SHINE EVER SO BRIGHTLY

The word "integrity," is an important word and concept. The meaning on dictionary.com explains it as this: "adherence to moral and ethical principles; soundness of moral character; honesty." It is very important I believe that we become people that use 'integrity, in our everyday lives. We need to use it in our personal lives and in our professional lives as well. We need to make it a way of life, because by doing so we make a better world and not just a world that moves from point A to point B with no thought or care for the outcome and how it will affect other people. We live on this planet with other people and doing what is right by all is what will move this world to a more peaceful loving place and a more respectful one as well.

The dictionary.com meaning of integrity states that we need to "adhere to moral and ethical principles." This is so important. The world is filled with amoral and unethical people that only care about themselves and their wants, needs and desires and forsaking all of humanity. I know I never want to be one of those people because I believe I have a conscience, one that stands for something strong and will go a long way.

In my life I always feel better when I know I've done the right thing in any given situation. Whether the reasons are perhaps a guilty conscience if I do it wrong, or I will get in trouble with the powers that be, or because I was taught right from wrong from my mother and want to do the best for all involved and the end result is what matters. In work, play or daily life, if you know something is not right, we have to stand up and say something and do something. I was a supervisor in a medical facility helping to run an office and felt it was my obligation when dealing with people's lives that I **always** had to get it right. I made sure that while I checked paperwork that the names were spelled correctly and that the age and personal information matched and was on the money. I made sure that the tests they would be taking matched to what went back to the technologist. It may be my job and what I am getting paid for, but knowing that these patients who are here for the reason of being sick or not feeling well, we cannot get it wrong and give them the wrong test which extends next to the wrong diagnosis. These are the reasons why I always have to make sure and double check and re-check my work.

As my superior and friend Concetta once said many years back when I started working with her and it rings true today, if two patients come in seeking medical testing and for arguments sake lets call them "Charlie and Jack" Jack who is sick, gets a "clean bill of health," and Charlie who is well gets a diagnosis that he has Cancer when he doesn't, and Jack thinking he is well and healthy going about his life unbeknownst that he could be dying. With this two lives can be ruined and the family members as well. This is why it is so important to never make these mistakes that can be so costly. I have always remembered this and use it in my work or in any similar situation. Yes, these people can be strangers, but what if it was us, or someone we loved that this circumstance happened to by someone else's hand. It is always important to show integrity in our work and in our lives.

    It is not just about being smart, because the world is filled with smart people. We need people who are caring and showing this caring through our actions, in how we work and present ourselves. We need to live and lead our lives with a good moral compass. Because when we do we can sleep nights, and look ourselves in the mirror and know we did the right thing. This doesn't mean that because we aim to get all things right that we hit the nail on the head each time and sometimes like I have learned, we could have hit it into left field and it could have cost us our jobs or someone's uncertain outcome, which I am thankful did not occur. I know I am blessed and never take my job for granted, even though it can be taxing many days.

I have always wondered how people in this world who do unethical things and with no morals can sleep at night, can look themselves in the mirror and not see deep inside the superficial façade that the mirror gives back to the person looking into that mirror.

The dictionary.com meaning continues by saying: "The soundness of moral character and honesty." I know by living my life that if we show integrity in our lives and we present and stand for a good moral character, by being honest with ourselves and what we do in our lives we then make our lives better, we encourage other lives, and can hopefully make this a guilt free world.

When we are young as teenagers, integrity is not part of our vocabulary or mindset since our immaturity is more a way of life for us at that point. Hopefully our parents are there to give us the guidance we will need to show us right from wrong and help change the course that might go from bad to worse if no one is paying attention. I know for me a guilty conscience always works. Hopefully in time as the years go by and we go from childhood into adulthood, integrity can become a part of our vocabulary and actions.

When I was in Jr. High School, I stole a Milky Way bar from a store and got caught doing it. I was scared, rightfully so. The owner wanted to know my name, address and what school I went to and I think I spilled everything and never came back again, or stole anything again. I was too scared and didn't want to go to jail. I can laugh about it now. As I grew I matured and learned to do what is right and live a life with integrity. I believe that all these little life experiences teach us and if we learn from them we don't make them again. If we don't learn from them the universe puts us back in the situation until we do. We then become adults and somewhere along the line, whether it is in our twenties, thirties or forties, we start to "get it," hopefully, though some never "get it," from day one till the end of their lives. When we start to get it, our minds have become more formed and what we are doing changes and our perspective is in a better more mature place. We start to know what is right when presented to us and take the necessary steps to make sure all goes well as best to our ability. This is what integrity is all about.

But there are some teenagers, and young men and women out there who if taught by their parents well do take things seriously and are responsible to do the right thing such as loving friends, Concetta and her sister Carmela that because they had wonderful loving parents who made sure they became the women they are today do have integrity and show it in their lives. So we can never make a blanket statement across all young people having no sense and being immature and doing completely stupid things. But I do believe that in any job we do, any life experience we are presented with, we must use some sort of integrity and responsibility to make sure things go well and when we do a better world this will be for one and for all.

"The most important gift to embrace in our world is our collective humanity, such as our family, friends, neighbors, co-workers, and our brothers and sisters in the world. This is so important because in the end all we truly have is each other in the world, everything else is secondary; money, possessions, etc. It's true that we need money to survive and pay the bills, BUT PEOPLE MUST COME FIRST. After people and money, it is okay to then have a few nice possessions, but people must come first and having and using integrity is where we consider people first in all our daily actions with them and each other."

"If we embrace integrity into our every day thinking, our lives will shine ever so brightly. This rings true because by consciously making choices from the prospective of 'how will this person feel, by my actions. Would this person be hurt by my thoughtless behavior? Am I only caring of how I come out at the end and with no sincere thought for others? How would I feel if I was treated in this manner?' If the answer from those questions is not from a feeling of wellness,' then we need to re-think and start to make choices with integrity, of making the right choice, the responsible choice which will make everyone feel like a winner and loss if any will be minimal."

"Having integrity means being responsible and making sure that everything will go right in any situation. Yes things can and will go wrong, but by thinking ahead and doing the best we can any problems that could occur will not come to fruition because we took precautions, and made sure everything would go the way it should. When we take on the responsibilities of taking care of children, a work situation, doing something important for someone else or even our own life situations, we need to use our smarts and integrity to make sure all goes well all the way to the end. We should never take on something that we know that will be too much for us to handle because someone could come back to us and say we should have done this better, and with more concern and care for what ever job or situation we undertook. So we should always know our limits and do our best."

"None of us on this planet are perfect people. We all make mistakes, do things that are not right and may at times hurt others. We rub people the wrong way as some do us. But we can always start over and forgive our mistakes and become better, brighter, more loving people. As long as we haven't infringed on the rights of others in such a way as to physically and mentally abuse someone to the point of no return we can always come back and begin again. We can start the following day on a bright new morning or at this very instant to become the people God would have us be and the type of people we should want to be. We still may have bad days where the world appears to not be our friend and going against us, but those times should only be few and far between. Once through them we should turn things around to become the best people we can possibly be."

"Impressions are important and I believe the impressions we want to leave children about ourselves are that they see us as "caring, loving souls." If they see us always in confrontations with other people it shows them a negativity that solves no problems but just puts clouds over relationships and this is what children will pick up and carry with them into adulthood. But if we also show them that the world is not perfect, but that we can make it a better one it should hopefully lead a lasting impression on our future societies which are our children and their children and so on."

"First impressions are valuable, but a second impression sometimes should not be ignored, if the first one fell like a dead balloon or circumstances happened beyond our control. Perhaps we were late due to an unfortunate set of circumstances, or perhaps we tripped on our words and thoughts during the interview process. Whatever those circumstances were it should not matter and if the powers that be are sincere, they will give us a second chance to show our value and what we can give to this new job or opportunity. They will express their integrity and allow a second chance for us to show our best."

"Doing what we know to be right even when the crowd may not go along with us is the way to go because we are thinking from our conscience, a place of integrity. People who feel bad doing something they know is wrong will want to right their wrong. In the end we will feel good deep within and the next time we face a similar situation we will know how to solve this issue...we will do it with integrity."

"Always do what is right, because the right way is always the best way. If we do the right thing, we can sleep nights and be able to look ourselves in the mirror guilt free, and isn't this the best feeling in the world? Using integrity in our everyday lives will give us this eternal feeling."

Chapter 7

CULTURE, RELIGION AND SPIRITUALITY

This world is filled with just fewer than 7 billion people. When it comes to culture, religion and spirituality, I feel that each of us perhaps come in five different categories as to the belief in God. Some come from one culture or another, a religious background that they may participate in or not, another perhaps doing daily spiritual practices, there are some who do not believe in anything, and the last is undecided, unsure of what to believe in. I personally live my life in the belief in God and live my life each day to include "spiritual practices."

What is more important; to be religious or to be a spiritual person? This question has probably been around for centuries with numerous answers and a debate which will continue on for centuries to come. One would say religion, while another would say it is important to be spiritual, while others who do not believe in anything and would soon as pray if they pray in the first place to a Ritz cracker box as my sister once pointed out about someone she knows. (By the way we love Ritz crackers and eat them all the time.)

I believe that it most certainly has to come from

the individual on how he or she needs to live their life. Some will choose their own religion, convert to another religion of their choice or find as I the writer of this book would choose to be and am a very spiritual person, devoting my time to numerous spiritual practices. There are many who do not believe in God or would not want to do with anything of a religious nature. We have people in all walks of life that may love God, and are devoted to Him and living a way of life that they feel would be on His level of thinking and experiencing, and others who will still lead a good decent life without the benefit of believing in God. Each has a belief and each has a right in this world to believe how they see fit.

    I know for me I am a person who believes in God and is devout in my beliefs and spiritual practices which are done each and every day. Each morning I rise and happily start the day as I will go to my spiritual corner which is my couch and get into a lotus position and close my eyes and pray and meditate. I quietly in my mind thank God for all the gifts and blessings He has bestowed upon me. They include my family and friendships, my home and job and how my life is and still can be. Asking Him to show me how I can make my life better and the lives of others better still. I ask him to help the homeless and the hungry, the jobless and for some we may find hopeless. I pray for peace in the world for one and for us all. It is some of the most rewarding times of my day and life to do this consistently each day. The best time I found to do this is when I wake up. I am spending time with God and feeling the peace and joy He gives me. It makes the rest of my day go more smoothly. Even if I had a bad day at the office once I get over the hump of the day and all is peaceful and quiet I know all will be well again.

Once I finish praying I open the workbook for "A Course in Miracles," and do the lesson for the day. It is a set of three books with the second volume being 365 days of workbook meditation exercises from which the text sets forth and I listen to the most beautiful speaking voice of spiritual teacher Marianne Williamson read the lesson and I do what the lesson is asking for and I would listen to the audio several times throughout the day. This book has changed my life. It is not a religion of any kind, but it does teach us to forgive and through forgiveness we obtain inner peace by using spiritual themes that are universal in nature. It was so powerful to me and it gave no restrictions and I found it to be filled with beautiful ideas and sweet poetic words. There are 365 days worth of mediation exercises. I have found that I could believe and do these meditations on a consistent daily basis and I look forward each day to a new exercise and doing what is asked of me and I do so lovingly.

I listen to a wonderful internet radio station called "Hay House Radio," started by its founder Louise Hay and she has wonderful people on this radio station, such as Doreen Virtue, Michael Neill, and Robert Holden and numerous others that have transformed my spiritual life to make it more meaningful and filled with depth. This has also led me to other audios and books on spirituality and they have changed my life for the better.

On Oprah back in the late nineties, the year 2000 and most of 2001 a great segment called "Remembering Your Spirit," which with sentimental background music people would tell their story about their life struggles and what they went through, then when they had hit rock bottom, how they found and/or rediscovered their spirit and rejuvenated it to a place that was more healthier, happier and more profound. It was something I found which was truly needed for myself and millions of others who have gone through tough life struggles and needed a way to get out. It was a segment that hit a cord with me and so many others, but not enough. Just one day before 9/11/2001, Oprah had stopped doing this segment; with no correlation to each other. I found out years later that people just weren't "getting it," and if ever a time we did need this was from 9/11 and beyond but it was not to be, but I always found it to be a very inspirational segment. I believe that there are so many great things to observe, enjoy and embrace in all cultures and religions. Celebrating the differences that make each culture and religious group special but also realizing that even though one may pray differently or celebrate differently we primarily all want the same things in this lifetime. We want to be happy and healthy and live in this world with family and friends and all our brothers and sisters in a joyous, peaceful and loving way, and each of us has earned this right as equal parts of humanity.

Coming from the religion of Judaism, I am very proud of my heritage as we all should be from what we were born into. I respect it and respect all who choose to follow it in their lives and want to make it a way of life for them and their families. I personally respect and love the history, culture and humanity side of Judaism; I just do not follow it in terms of a religious nature. It wasn't coming from an innate part of my heart but I found another way to love and respect God.

Personally I feel that whether we choose any one of the great religions, or just a spiritual practice we should choose something. We should be a part of something that brings us to our knees in surrender to the All-Knowing and All-Powerful Man upstairs. He gave us the "gift of life," and we should find some way of honoring that. I personally fall into the category of spiritual practice in my daily life and world. Whether for me or anyone wanting to go deeper into their lives we may find it through prayer and meditation, yoga, lighting candles and incense or making our environment peaceful and more loving for ourselves and each other; because this is how we set up the universe for treating us back. I know for me that I was always spiritual in some form or another but once I was in my thirties and forties I had been through depression and sadness, pain and anxiety that I knew becoming more spiritual was the way to go and I searched out different spiritual paths. I was reading books and listening to audios, as I mentioned above finding Hay House internet radio and also Oprah Radio, this is where I found spiritual teacher Marianne Williamson again, and this time for a whole year she spoke about and taught about the principles in "A Course in Miracles." I also embraced everything to do with happiness, gratitude and kindness.

I know that there are others in this world that do not believe in God and have no interest or belief in any type of faith. I find this really sad, but each of us has a right to choose or not to choose how we live our lives and what faith we do or do not follow. Discovering spirituality for me has been so profound that I wonder how others can find having none is the way to go. To toss it up in the air and say that bad things in life is "just the way things are," is not a valid answer and seems so depressing and final and we are in a no-win situation. I do not believe in that way of thinking and I believe no one wants to believe that way in their heart of hearts, but to each his own.

It is very important to entice our spirit and let it out and experience our divine selves. Once it is out we must tune it up and daily rejuvenate it to become the best part of ourselves. I know for myself I have become for the better a very devout person in my spiritual practices. Each day I am doing my prayer and mediation session with God, thanking him for all the blessings and gifts He has bestowed on me and my loved ones. I feel this is very important for me and this makes me a much more peaceful and loving man. I have said "goodbye," to the boy I was, the man I was and "HELLO," to the man I am, hope to be and will be in this lifetime and then in spirit.

God I believe wants us to know and remember Him and never forget Him and definitely NOT fear Him. He let us have "free will," but only to become the best part of humanity that we can be in His likeness. We need to be kind and compassionate, caring, loving, peaceful and empathic people to ourselves and to each other equally. He is an "All Knowing," and "All Loving," God, not an "I WANT YOU TO FEAR ME GOD." So I do not fear Him, and have felt this in my spiritual practices and how I live my life with a good moral compass is the life HE wants for me.

It is however unfortunate that there are many people in the world that use the name of God and all that He holds dear to create injustice, evil and destruction on the world and its people instead of letting each of us be allowed to live in peace and harmony with each other and to "live and let live." Even though there are people out there who will both hijack a beautiful religion, turn, twist and re-write it so when all is said and done we all wonder what the religion was originally.

Yet with all this, there are people out there who are genuinely good, and care about others and are willing to put goodness into the world and bless all of humanity by doing the "right thing," and "helping others." I hope I am one of those people as well as all who are reading this book. "Good must triumph over evil" and it is our jobs to do this.

So in the end whatever we choose for ourselves, whether we enjoy a certain culture that we want to participate in, join a religion because we want to be a part of something with meaning. We want to begin any spiritual practice that takes us deeper and makes us more healthier, more loving, more peaceful people and what will happen is we will have a world where we all work together and live side by side in harmony. I wish it for me and I wish it for all us, unity, love for all of brother and sisterhood. Amen.

"Love and appreciate GOD or your HIGHER spirit. Be thankful and grateful for this life and ALL the BLESSINGS it holds."

"Having different religions, cultures, different types of people on this earth is a good thing, because we can share in everyone's gifts."

"We should all respect other people's religious beliefs, even if it is foreign to us and they in turn will and should show respect to ours. Each belief may seem different on the surface, but deep down, we all want the same things: Love, friendship, kindness, peace and happiness in this lifetime for ourselves, family, friends, fellow human beings and future generations."

"For some people being religious is important and for others it is important to become spiritual. Choose your path and flourish my sisters and brothers."

"Have an open heart and become a free spirit. We need to rid ourselves of our lower selves and become our highest and brightest selves. When we do others will follow."

"If we want to share in other people's cultures, religious holidays, etc, we should get to know our own and where we came from first. Then we can share the beautiful gifts each culture has to offer. By not knowing where we came from short changes us and others, so when we have learned where we came from the seeking out of other cultures and their history will be much sweeter for us all."

"Each day make some time for the practice of prayer and meditation. This can and is so liberating and freeing."

"Never count out three important healing tools of the many that we have: the power of prayer and meditation and the power of music. These three can be insightful and give us the breath of fresh air our lives need day to day, during the conflict or craziness known as 'life.' The results of the power of prayer, mediation and music can be the greatest services we can give to ourselves and to humanity. So we should employ them in our worldly work and then watch the magical gifts of life return to us in full awareness and glory…Amen."

Chapter 8

RACISM SHOULD NEVER EXIST

Why do we hate? What is it inside some of us, many of us that makes race, the color of someone's skin, the culture they came from or sexual orientation that makes others treat us as less than human. Why do some people choose to see others with contempt and use it as a reason, to belittle, make fun of, disrespect and even cause bodily harm in the form of violent acts, which can and has led to death? This is the taking of a life for no reason except for the simple act of dislike for someone that it turns to hate and rage, violence and of death.

All through the ages, we have seen wars and violent acts committed against humanity. Even to this day in the twenty-first century hate is as active and full-blown as it was from day one when the beginnings of war descended upon us all, set up shop and has never left and just grows like a CANCER.

To quote the famous but true words by Rodney King "Can't we all... just...get along?" To hate someone for the color of their skin, what country or culture they originated from or whom they love is simply and utterly and totally wrong. The segment of humanity who celebrates hatred by committing anything from small comments to crimes of violence and death against humanity should at the very least be ashamed of themselves.

I believe that racism can come in many forms and whether it is in subtle forms (such as a comment: "Those black people are lazy," or "all Russian people are pushy,") as opposed to saying which I believe to be okay "This person is lazy," or "that patient in the doctor's office is pushy." Even worse full blown racism and hatred such as murder, and the wiping out of a group of people. Racism is racism and it should NEVER be tolerated. It should be spoken up against as best as we can for that given moment and or time. Sometimes for whatever reason we may not be able to stand up on a soap box and preach about how wrong hatred against a race can be because it might put us in bodily harm at that moment, but if you can say something or do something I believe we must and should.

How sad to think that there are people out there with the mindset of hating others, or doing harm to others because the color of their skin, the people whom they innately love, or come from a part of the world that seems different and even strange to you or me. Who are we to put someone down because they come from a different background or speak a different language?

Didn't we ever think that perhaps that person has something important to teach us, or we to teach them in an honest loving way. Can we not remember that we all feel pain, and all need love and nurturing? We want the best for ourselves and our families, and all other groups of people want and deserve the same. We need to be kinder, more loving to one another and embrace the so called "differences," that make us unique and special. Yes, there may be a difference, but do we not stop to think that this could be a good thing. A world filled with people all looking the same, dressing the same and acting the same would make for such a boring, dreary world. Nothing would be different; we'd all be talking in monotone voices, walk the same way and we couldn't tell each other apart, because we'd all be the same.

I believe that we are all taught on some level to hate others or to love others when we are small by parents, and others who come in contact with us. Because if we put children from all different backgrounds and races together in a room they innately want to shine and just be themselves. They want to play and laugh together. They do not care about issues of race, hate, disrespectful language or disregard about others and wanting to do away with others unless adults teach and nurture hatred.

I believe that some adults are teaching children to

hate and show distain to others. They then nurture this to the extent that kids grow up with hardened and unloving hearts because of what their parents behavior displayed to them. These children grow up into adults believing others are inferior to them and they believe it with every fiber of their being. Someone who doesn't act, think, dress, look like them in every way must be sub-human and not worthy of a life of happiness, joy, peace and respect. They hate other races believing they are inferior to them or just because someone feels love toward someone and innately wants to love them and be loved by that person of the same sex, then who is someone to say it is wrong, vile, goes against God and humanity. Anything that goes against love, friendship, kindness, and compassion for all people truly goes against God and humanity. We need to look within ourselves and find the true essence of kindness and love for one another and then embrace it and express it to others.

    I believe that it is okay to dislike the individual from any race, creed or so forth if they are disrespectful, hateful, or harmful to others, because there is good and bad in people in this world, but we cannot blame a whole group of people or hurt them and call them by disrespectful names and violate their existence because of a few people, this is just wrong and should never be tolerated. I always stand up against bigotry and hateful words and we all should as well. If we do not do it for others, then who will be there for us when people start to call us hurtful names and want to do us bodily harm. Always be a person who shows kindness, friendship, love, caring and respect to others. If we do the right thing, it will be returned to us because the universe is always watching and would we not want to show that we know the right way by doing the right thing.

As we know Dr. Martin Luther King Jr. was one of the great leaders who fought for civil rights and against racism and I hope to leave a statement of my life by following his lead and stop bigotry and racism in any way I can. I hope to do this through my writings, knowing what is right and fighting for what is wrong and doing it through the art of peace and of love. I will do it by standing up and always speaking out and saying something to the person or persons who are bigoted or express racist comments. I will do it and encourage us all to do it and make this a better world. I know through experience that I could not live with myself if I said or did nothing to fight bigotry and racism. I just could not.

In the course of my life I have stood up to someone at work who had made bigoted and racist comments about any group of people they did not like at the moment. Making inappropriate comments about a group of people is ALWAYS wrong. Making a comment about one individual sans their skin color, ethnicity or sexual orientation is okay, because it is about that person only. It is about how they treat their family, their friends, and strangers from all parts of the world who are our brothers and sisters. We in the end are all the same. Show respect and kindness for what each person represents is what is important. I hope some of my feelings and ideas that follow will resonate with many people to take a stand and not accept bigotry. We need to become part of the solution and not part of the problem, if we do so then as the song goes "What a wonderful world this would be." That is the world I want to join and live in...don't we all? We can start today, this minute, this instant to make this world a more loving world and peaceful world for all by wiping out bigotry and racism. It is the world we all deserve and one I want to see in my lifetime and I know you do as well. Amen.

"Racism is never healthy; in subtle forms or in FULL FORCE. To say negative thoughts in private or to the world about one race, creed or sexual-orientation does not lift us up to our highest selves, but brings us down to our lowest forms of humanity. We want a healthy world where we share it with everyone; and all racism projects is an unhealthy world where hate only breeds hate. What we need to replace it with is A WORLD WHERE LOVE BREEDS LOVE."

"If someone says something racist, call them on it. Don't let them get away with it. Because if one day it turns out to be said about our race, creed, color or sexual orientation, we would want someone to stand up for us."

"Children learn to be racist because they are taught this. Teach love instead and watch a more BEAUTIFUL person grow."

"We should never be made to feel that we are less than anyone else. We are special because we are alive on this earth. We are special because we were chosen to live and breathe on this planet. No matter in what form…race, creed, color or sexual orientation we were blessed to be born into, each person has the right to be respected and loved for who and what they are, and who they can become. We never disrespect others because what our eyes see. Beauty is deep down and there can be beauty in people by their actions and how they speak about and treat others. We should never make blanket statements about whole groups of people. If there are individuals that have less than wholesome qualities and hurt others no matter what they look like they should be admonished. So always be a person who respects all kinds of people. No matter where we go in this world there are different groups of people who on the surface look different from us, but in some cases we could be the one who is different on the surface to them as well and be falsely judged. So we need to treat and respect people for our commonalties as well as ours differences and know we all come from the same Loving God."

Chapter 9

WORLD PEACE AND HUMANITY

World peace should be the main goal of and for all of humanity. If people would stop listening to their ego minds and start listening to what is in their hearts, then the road to recovery from war and destruction to universal world peace would start to make sense. How could it not? We were not born to hate and fight, and destroy our fellow man, woman and child.

Yet, we find that is the main goal for so many cruel inhuman and barbaric individuals who have no need or compassion for others. Greed, power, and cruel hearts can and have led to the downfall of many nations and the "ethnic cleansings," of many sections of humanity.

Tears fall from my eyes and sadness fills my heart knowing that as I write this and lead my life moment to moment and day by day, that cruelty lives and breathes in the hearts and minds of so many people. Not only do they not just keep it inside but they make a plan of action that all the evil that lives in their hollow hearts come to fruition to destroy our loving world.

Since time began there have been wars started by

people who wanted power over others, to dominate a people to do and act and live with as the war mongers saw fit and had no care and concern for what the people wanted for themselves. There would be one ruler and the rest would do as the ruler wanted.

This happened with The Pharaoh and the Hebrews as Moses came to help them. The evil of the Nazi's in Germany proclaiming all Jews as evil and nonentities, and with this they would throw babies out of windows, shoot men, women and children with guns, put them in gas chambers, and into the ovens. Killing off as many Jews, so as to wipe them all out this way and so there would be no Jews in the future or generations to come.

For the past 66 years since the Jews have been gifted land in the Middle East along with the Palestinians to live side by side and we have seen not nations coming together, but people further apart from peace and happiness. There is just more fighting and less love and peace. This is a great sadness for me and so many others that instead of coming together for the greater part of humanity we are pulling further apart and rewriting a world in such a way that we will and have become a separate place and not a world of caring and sharing individuals.

How about we the American people taking the land away from the Native American Indians? We came here and couldn't have cared less about the people already here. We took over the land as our new home and instead of asking to share the land with love and affection we killed and harmed so many and we just didn't care who we hurt, we just took over the land, made it our own with no concern with anyone who was here first.

How about the African American experience: How horrible to have been forcibly taken away from their tribal homes by evil men who put them to work to become slaves with no dignity and pride. They were taken from their families and when they created their own families in which this way they were forced to have future generations become slaves, the slave owners could break up these families, never to be seen from again. How cruel is this? In today's world, we have seen ethnic cleansing in places such as Rwanda, Kosovo, and now Darfur. There seems to never be a rest from war, hate and evil.

I believe in my heart that in order to have world peace we have to apologize to all the people we have hurt, harmed, killed and tried to eradicate as a nation and as a world.

We have to make amends and pay back what we took. It may not be so easy to give back the land to the

Native American Indians but we must first apologize and see and do what is fair and right. We American's must apologize to the Jews who were sent back to Germany on the ships they came on only to be exterminated during the Holocaust years. We must apology to the African Americans who built America with sweat and tears, followed by the Jim Crow years and how evil people could show themselves to be. Not being able to look a white person in the eye because black people were looked on as inferior and to lynch a black man or any man was an evil act and wearing white sheets to cover one's self was a cowardice act back in the day and still is in many parts of racist territory today. An apology first is what is needed and what should be sincerely expected.

Once this is done and restitution in some form is paid, we need to rebuild and embrace peace, and love and help each other and make this world what it was meant to be which is to shine brightly. The light in all of us must shine through and with that a calm peace will take over and we then give it back to the universe and then we can all join together and be the best part of humanity. This is not idealistic thinking, this I believe can and will happen if we give it a chance.

I know when I look within my heart I can find happiness and peace living and breathing there. I then pray for it for my family and my friendships, my home and my community. I feel it then spreads to others and this is how world peace can begin. It then can spread across the land to different parts of the globe to different people, I believe that in the end spreading peace and love all over the world we can begin to see the seeds of world peace toward humanity grow into something so very wonderful. This alone should be our goals, peace and love, not war and death.

    One of the best opportunities that I feel helps humanity and world peace is by doing charity walks. I have done the "MS Walks," and "Aids Walk NY," and the fact that there is a cause where we need to fight to find a cure and we come together by donating money and then coming together for a walk. I see it as a walk in "unity." We are coming together to walk in one direction, with a cause and together show our support in the common goal of eradicating something dreadful as any disease can give to find a cure. This is humanity at its finest. I feel great knowing that I got some checks together and go on the walk that will help other people who are fighting a dreadful disease, because we all know that person could be us or someone we love dearly and we must all help one another.

    During the awful day of 9/11/2001 when both World Trade Towers fell and thousands of lives were lost as two planes as guided missiles caused this devastation, a third in The Pentagon in Arlington Virginia, and Flight 93 being shot down in Shanksville Pennsylvania, and all the days to follow, humanity was also at its finest. We all came together to help each other and help to heal one another in a time so horrific it would break all our hearts. The only thing now is that we have to continue helping one another, stop the fighting and the wars and bring peace to the world and humanity to the foreground of life. We can do it in times of crisis as we have seen in the past and now we must do it for times when things are good, if that can be said. We must stop war and bring back peace and love to the world and the beauty of humanity will be its reward.

How great is that? Just by doing what we can is just the seeds needed to begin what is lacking in this world, such as love, kindness, caring and compassion along with giving friendship to all that we meet. We have to be the conduits for peace and love and friendship in order to have world peace begin, continue and change the world in what it should and can be. Just by changing our perceptions, our attitudes and our loveless thinking will the world begin to change and a more loving world will come to fruition. It is on you, me and all of us for the future of the planet and its children. We need to leave this world a more loving world for all and it is our individual and collective responsibility to achieve this. So let us start right now, this second, this minute and this very hour of the day. Godspeed, angel blessings, peace, love, and Amen.

"As individual people living on this planet, we must be conduits for love and peace for the planet and its people. We must pray for world peace, and then take action toward it. We take action by becoming caring loving people, giving service to others and by starting at this point other people will follow us and with it world peace has begun."

"World peace can only start with us. We must create a healthy loving spiritual environment in our home and work place for this to happen. Then extend it out to all the people we meet and come in contact with. Remember it all begins with us and once this has begun the vibration of world peace has been set in motion."

"I believe in order to have peace and love on this earth we need to first apologize to the many groups of people in this world who have been persecuted, and murdered by evil, and cruel sadistic leaders and their followers from the past and present day. We must apologize in the United States of America for slavery and to all the ancestors of African Americans who help build this nation from the sweat on their brow and for no pay. We must also apologize to the Native Americans who lived here first whose land was taken from them. This includes the people who lost loved ones to the genocide that befell Rwanda and Darfur. Once we have done this I believe it is a starting point for us all to begin to heal and move forward and build on a world where peace will truly begin. That is the group I want to join. The group I want to be apart of, where we right the wrongs of the past by apologizing and starting over fresh. We then can start the building of a brighter future by learning from the past and leaving the mistakes of the past behind, see where we can go from there. It is our future and our children's and we have to respectfully do what is right. If we don't we will never heal and we remain stagnant."

"Become someone who brings others to their higher selves. We never want to become someone who puts or pulls others down. We should find only the good in others, help them to bring it out in themselves and hopefully they will pay it forward. Doing anything less will only bring out a negativity that does no one any good. We were all meant to shine and when we bring out the best in each other we will shine ever so brightly. These are just some of seeds that build our humanity and peaceful encounters with each other will be its reward."

"Each person has gifts. We need to use those gifts so we don't lose them and along with using our gifts to make the world a better place be the one who brings out the gifts in others."

"Be thankful to have the ability to make choices (many people around the world do not). Some areas around the globe people are forced to do what they do not want to do. Others make the choices for them not caring what they like, want or desire in this world. So when we have the right and ability to make 'choices,' know that we are blessed and be thankful for this 'right'. We should use our 'choices' with care and responsibility for who they would and could affect."

"The planet earth is ours and we must take care of it and respect it. It is our responsibility not to pollute it with garbage and evil. The future generations deserve it as we deserve it.

"Choose peace over war, love over hate and construction over destruction. When we do, the purist essence of who we are can and will come to the light. If we choose to live our lives this way it will give others permission to live their lives the same way with the positive choices they make."

"If we learn to 'love,' instead of 'hate,' wars will end. Wars may not end on a global level at first, but if it starts on the level of us and those around us, then one day there will be fewer wars and more love in this world. The beautiful idea of 'make love, not war,' is a great sentiment to live by and practice for. We want our future generations to be here in one piece and live for peace, and come into the world that is filled overflowing with love, not overflowing hatred for people with opposite views, different skin color, religion or who we naturally choose to love. We want the future generations to flourish and we must be the generation to begin it because passing the buck wears thin and we will never help peace and love flourish on the earth."

"Become a person that builds things up and not a person who tears them down. We need a world with more love, and respect for people, places and things. We need more creativity in this world. We need artists who draw or paint; people who shoot photography of the beauty in this world, singers who sing exquisite arias or love songs, and people who want to make a difference in this world so it will be better than when we found it. Let each of us become that valuable someone and may the future of our world be brighter and more loving because of us…Amen."

Chapter 10

VOLUNTEERING AND HELPING OTHERS

The greatest gift to humanity we can give is the gift of ourselves coming together to help, and care for each other. In a sense in this world, on this planet while living here we are essentially all we have. We are all God's children whether we come from different backgrounds, races, creeds, or sexual orientations; we are all individually and collectively, "the children of God." I believe such as through my own life we need to act like "the children of God," and always be willing to help one another and be there in whatever way that is most needed for any situation.

My goal in this life and worldly level in which I see as my divine life purpose is to be a "great writer," and a "great humanitarian." It is something I feel in my blood and know in my soul that these are the directions my life is set to lead in whatever way it will follow. I believe this has been since birth and is my path to fulfill and I want to do so lovingly. I want and know I can use them both together and separately in whatever way is best for all.

Hopefully, as I have said before that in my writings I hope I can say many things or something specific that can change a person's life for the better. Perhaps I can give them hope and promise or encouragement and inspiration in a place that might not have existed in the past for them or that they might have lost along the way through whatever life circumstances brought them to the place they found themselves in. Life can bring us so low sometimes that we wonder how we can get out. It might be a long journey to get to the place that we all need to get to, but perhaps because of what I said in my writing to make someone feel better, think differently or see a brighter way that my life will have been worth living and so will theirs. Maybe they found a person's story which is close to theirs in resemblance inspiring to make better choices, how wonderful for them and for me or the person who gave them the inspiration. This is truly enlightening.

    I know for me as I have said before through my depression, pain and anxiety in the past how others inspired me to get out of depression and help me to see the sunshine in life that was clouded over for what seemed the longest time. Great teachers such as Marianne Williamson, His Holiness the Dalai Lama, Doreen Virtue, Louise Hay and others have put that sunshine back for me and I want to pay it forward back into the universe. This is where my writing comes in as others did for me and this is also where "my humanitarianism," "my wanting to help others," comes in to play.

I love to help others, I believe I always have and will until the day I pass on back into spirit. I just know that helping people is the "right thing to do," and I say why not? Why would we not want to be "a blessing" on someone else's life?

In October 2012, we saw the devastation of what Hurricane Sandy did to the Northeast. High winds roared like never before and floods filled homes so high people felt their lives in danger and some even lost their homes. I know close people who lost a lot, and yet they are thankful because they have each other, because with what they faced other people lost their lives. Some had nowhere to go, and became displaced. It was a horrible event for the east coast. With this horrible event that no one deserves to bear, it was wonderful to see the world coming together to help in whatever form was necessary, in any way we could. Was it enough, could I or we do more for them? It is a question that's easy to ask when some didn't lose more than electricity but we always have to help. We can all do our parts. While many of us can send our prayers and sincere wishes, and money, many can help tear down the rooms and homes to help rebuild and provide clean food and water and aid. It a beautiful experience when we see people helping others. As the months go on, are their lives a little easier, scared from the experience perhaps, but somewhat getting back to norm? It is hard to say, because things take time.

    As I mentioned above, sometimes if all one person can do such as send prayers and some money then that is the right action and we are "part of the solution," not "part of the problem." While there are others in the world that can take larger actions they too are helping. Everything counts, it is when we close our eyes not to look over and ignore the problems do we become apart of the problem and that is the real sadness.

    Back on September 11, 2001 and the days and months that followed, we came together as a nation and helped to heal the open wounds of all the death and destruction that came from that horrific day and event that will never be forgotten. The people in the World Trade Towers, the Pentagon, the planes which were the missiles for the devastation and the people of lower Manhattan experienced what we could never imagine. All the people from all around the nations that came to help us in our hour of need shows genuine love and friendship. When in our worst hours we can find that we step up as loving people has shown us at our finest hour. This is what people should be about. We gave help and we gave our time and effort. The best of humanity came out to do its best to help us recover from this tragedy and it was wonderful.

    I know in my life I have always looked for ways to

help others. I do so with a combination of ways such as sending prayers, sending money, through my writings and "getting my hands dirty," as I like to say and go out there and help others. I have been on numerous charity walks such as "MS," "AIDS Walks," and "Diabetes Walk,". I know it is so important to find causes such as these and others. We were all there to fight a cause. We are all walking in one direction in unity to raise money and awareness and to find cures for diseases that we all may have, or could still have in the future. I walk these "Walks," because I know I am doing something valuable and important. I may someday be one of the people that I walk for and by my doing this I hope others will walk for me if the time came.

There are so many people, who do great things on a large scale such as Oprah and other wealthy philanthropists, but you and I can do great things too but perhaps on a smaller scale, but it is just as important that we still do things to help no matter how small, because it all makes a difference.

I know through experience and hope it will always ring true for me and I hope the reader of this work, that giving and helping, being a friend and volunteering our time and effort will we not just make for a better society, we will make for better people, the individual and as a whole. It is this positive energy that makes us create a better world. We should always give back to this world through any way we can and in the end we will have made a world of difference.

"Be a Volunteer; help your family, a friend, and all brothers and sisters alike. We should never discriminate in who we help. The simple fact that a person needs help should be enough. Just be the one to give it."

"When we help strangers there is an extra value in this: By helping a stranger we manifest in showing the universe and our higher power, God who we truly are and can become as spiritual beings on this planet. This lets the human race know we care and they feel good and so do we. This is a win-win situation. Any situation that is a win-win is always the best."

"Become a mentor or a teacher to someone and guide them."

"Find a cause that hits your heart and volunteer to help find a solution."

"Give donations to different charities. Choose ones that have meaning for you for different reasons and please give."

"In this life I have learned that it is important that we search for people and important causes to believe in with our hearts and souls. Once found we should fight in some way to help these people and the causes that speak to us. There is lack in the world and if we can give of our time, money and energy to fill that lack, our greatest purpose will start to be fulfilled."

"The kindness of strangers is a real deal. Be one of those 'kind strangers,' and help others."

"When we help strangers (our brothers and sisters) and the like, this in the end will leave us with nothing more than a satisfaction that we made a difference in the lives of others; and is this not the purpose of our lives?"

"Giving is so very important. While we think we have little and we think we don't have much to give, just think of the many people that have 'NOTHING,' and so I believe and as I have done through my own actions is to find it in my heart to dig a little deeper into my pockets and give a little more to others who truly have 'NOTHING.' This is what I hope and believe makes us better people."

Chapter 11

RESPECTING OTHERS, AS WE WOULD WANT OTHERS TO RESPECT US

As the famous quote reads: "Do unto others as you would have them do unto you," goes back a long way and I know still holds true today. We all want to be treated with respect, and by giving and showing respect do others in return give us the respect we ask for. If we treat others with distain and with lack of respect, we too will receive it coming back at us. Who wants to be treated with lack of respect or unkindly? Not I, nor you I'm sure. So what do we do as individuals who are looking for these concepts of respect, courtesy and friendliness? We give it to others in our daily journey. At home, at work, and at play we should always put our best foot forward, but we must put our best foot forward genuinely and sincerely.

Showing respect to others is vitally important to our human race and to the world we live in. Respect for ourselves and others is what should be in our mindset as we move along the path of our individual and collective journeys. If blessed enough, we learn respect, the giving and receiving of it by our parents, guardians and extended family members. They show us how to think and act toward ourselves and others.

There is so much unkindness in the world because of the lack of respect in how some may treat us or how we treat them and this includes us on a global level too not just our own small environment. Wars start and grow larger than life because of how we treat one another as if we do not matter in any form. There is no respect shown to the human race when we carelessly go about our ways as separate people, walking and living our separate lives as if we are fragments that have no whole parts. And so if we disrespect one another it doesn't matter, because my disrespecting you or anything I do against you doesn't affect me in any way or vice versa. Sadly it does and this kind of thinking is so wrong. We are not separate individuals walking separate lives despite what our eyes tell us, unless we choose to believe that. I do not choose to see us separate but I choose to see our "oneness," our "wholeness," and our "unity," and I know billions upon the world want to and do see that as well.

Whether at home, work, or play, we must align ourselves with respect for ourselves and others and a more peaceful loving world will come to fruition.

In one of the apartment houses I lived in, I always gave respect to the landlord face to face, or in how I treat the home in which I live. I work I pay my rent on time or paid just before the due date, I respect the apartment by keeping it clean and not destroying the apartment or break things in any way if you will. Responsible people do not do those things that would remove themselves from their home by doing the wrong thing. But respect is and should be a two-way street aka...mutual respect. Since I pay my rent on time, and take care of the apartment, my respect is there. From the perspective of the landlord, he or she wants a tenant, who pays their rent on time and respects the apartment and any rules that the landlord had wanted to input. With these win-win situations in what is really a business relationship the landlord should show and have respect for their tenant, which are the people who are in truth helping to pay their mortgage. Nevertheless, from the perspective of my landlord, he or she never seems to see it that way. They choose to think with greed and of themselves and what they can get out of someone else in whatever form that may be. Sadly, there is no concern for feelings or respect for another person, but themselves.

    There are two ways to build any and all relationships I've discovered. We can build them lovingly on solid ground and rock, or we can build it on sand. With solid ground and rock, any difficulties will hold up the relationship because the relationship was built on a foundation and surface that was strong and solid, aka love and mutual respect. We smile and laugh and the relationship will be healthy and happy, as all relationships should be. When built on sand however, the slightest disagreement or lack of mutual respect can and will disintegrate it since the relationship was built on sand by one or both persons seeking for personal gain.

Not knowing who I was on the first day I moved in my landlord in a shady way, while all was in disarray wanted to know if he too could have a cable box for his family through my contract. Just moving in and everything including my mind was in disarray, I said yes, but I didn't feel right about it, because it wasn't right. When we are just getting to know one another we do not ask for things that we should not be asking for. We are strangers at that moment and by asking for things, we aren't ingratiating ourselves to others, only leaving a sour taste in ones mouth about a potentially new relationship. The next thing he promised me was a two-year lease at a certain price and as the weeks moved on it never materialized. Each time I saw him his answer each time was different: don't worry… next week… next month… not to worry I will give it to you." It was always a different answer, and never one of truth or sincerity or mutual respect to build the relationship on solid ground and rock, only on sand. One year later the rent went up, still no lease and the relationship continued on building on sand.

When Super Storm Sandy in 2012 arrived, he did not care much about his tenant's welfare to come to see how we were doing. While our food in the fridge spoiled, he took care of his family by getting a generator to keep his lights on and food staying fresh. These and other countless examples with no mutual respect displays how the relationship continues to be built on sand and never coming close to being built on solid ground and rock the way all relationships should be built.

On my side I always chose to still build the relationship on solid ground and rock, despite the other person choosing to build it on sand, because two wrongs don't make a right as we all know, they only make things worse. So what do we do when there is no mutual respect and the relationship has been built on sand? We tend to avoid that person as much as possible, because of how they treated us, which doesn't help the situation.

One might ask then why did you stay and live there if there was no mutual respect between you and the landlord? The answer being, sometimes we cannot afford to move. In my case, the apartment was a great apartment and it was close to work and the rent I could afford. The bigger blessing that materialized was that I didn't have to see him much or at all.

We want to build loving relationships with all kinds of people that walk the world with us, family, friends, neighbors, co-workers and all brothers and sisters of the world. Unfortunately, we cannot be liked by everyone and vice-versa, but we can still adhere to the golden rule and I believe me must if we want our world to grow, blossom and prosper into the world that God intended from the beginning of all His creation.

At work we meet different kinds of people. Some we get along with and work well together and there are others who we don't get along with unfortunately, but we still try and get along with them. We still must adhere to the Golden rule. When our co-workers have family members who come to see them for whatever reason we too must be and show courtesy to them. Because not being courteous to their family members is being discourteous to our co-worker and we never want to do that, we would be creating so much more problems than we need or would want to create. So respect in all places, home, work and play are vitally important for our human race to find peace and prosper in healthy loving ways.

In my private life, I have a special needs friend named Eric. He is in his thirties and through a chance meeting at dinner with my family and his family we eventually became friends. We get together twice a month and we either go to a local pizza place or a local diner and enjoy a meal and talk and then we come back to my house and we watch the classic TV shows and movies. I am so happy we are friends and we get together because we all, "need," friends and when we see someone who needs a friend we should be their friend and invite them into our lives, which is the meaning of life and friendship. I feel great inside because I am doing something nice (never out of pity or self-interest,) but because it is the right thing and the nice thing to do and Eric I know is happy to have something we all want, need and should have which is a caring, loving friend. We never do things out of pity or self-interest because people with "special needs," or anyone else doesn't need our pity, only our love and friendship."

    Doing nice things for others and to others is so important because by doing so, we are making the recipient feel good inside and respected and that good feeling releases endorphins and the good feelings go all over our body. The endorphins will travel from the brain making its way all through the body thereby increasing the good feelings that will make us become healthier and more loving human beings. We will appear healthier and livelier around people because by doing good things for others we in return find it being reflected back to us in ways we can never have imagined.

Respecting others as we would want others to respect us means just this and all that much more, from me to you and you to me and all other people. I have also felt that to just "tolerate others," is unacceptable because it truly says, "I have no choice to be here next to you as a neighbor, co-worker or co-citizen and even though I have to accept it, it is still against my will, I won't like it, and that is that." But what this also shows that this "just tolerating," others, will come out in our feelings and dealings with others, then where is the respect that we have talked about? Yes, I admit it is not always easy to be loving and show respect to others who show no love or respect back to us. I get it and I understand it from both sides. I just want us not to fall short as loving human beings. I too have been in situations where a co-worker or neighbor after dealings with them that were not so pleasant moved into the mode of disrespect or non-trust. I know that there is work to do even if it is only coming from one side, my side to make the situation as pleasant as possible.

Respect must be earned from us to others and from others to us if we are going to have a decent if not a healthy loving relationship with others in the human race. I believe we need to transcend from "disrespect and just tolerating others," to that of "being as nice as we can and embracing others," in the highest possible way that we know how. We do know how and we must apply that knowing into action.

"Respecting others as we would want others to respect us," is a great concept that in the end everyone is feeling great and this is the feeling that we should want in our lives. It is the vitality, energy and youthfulness that comes from respecting each other, enjoying each others company and what we can do for each other makes us better human beings.

We don't have to love or even like everyone who comes into our path or space, as they do not have to like or love us, but at least try to show common courtesy and a pleasant demeanor. We can feel the good or negative energy emanating from the other person even though we haven't said anything to each other. When the feelings are happy and energetic we too can feel it with no words being said.

Respecting others as we would want others to respect us also applies to God, the angels, the universe, the environment, the earth, nature and animals as well. We all want respect and we all deserve respect and should be given it. First, we all deserve respect as living and breathing beings. When we accord respect we will receive the respect right back and when we do not give respect others will sadly not give it to us. So I hope and pray we give it to one another lovingly and if we made mistakes today, God willing we will have tomorrow to correct them.

    So I sincerely feel as a people, nation, and world we should always do our best because when doing and living with the concept of "Respecting others as we would want others to respect us," then great and wonderful things will come into our everyday lives. It is the "magic of humanity," and it comes from within and we just have to be gentle and kind to others and that magic will shine brightly in all we do and then from those around us. Always live the creed "Respect others as we would want others to respect us," and watch the miracles happen.

"We must never be "a people who just tolerates others." We must respect and love others because it is the right thing to do. No matter what group of people we come from we deserve to be appreciated. Acceptance is the way it should be. Tolerating someone just means that we do not show acceptance, love or caring for that person or group of persons. Tolerating someone else means just that I have 'no choice,' about the situation I am forced into so I will just try and live with it. What this shows about us is that we are being very disrespectable to another human being and we are at our lowest form of humanity. When we give love, respect, kindness and compassion to another human being we are attaining our highest selves and this is how we were meant to live."

"All groups of people on this planet are equal. No matter what race, skin color, sexual orientation, or culture we are born into, finding love should never be a set standard of falling in love, or marry 'our own kind,' because those ideas and beliefs are old fashioned, tired thinking and which needs to be reevaluated. We should be able to 'fall in love,' and 'marry,' whomever we fall in love with. We should be able to be with a person who is of a different color than we are, or from a different culture than we are, especially if both want to be together and both are consenting adults. Society and the world as a whole should let each person choose who they 'fall in love with,' 'want to be with,' or 'marry,' without family members or others who have no business being in other people's love life, to just let them be. 'Live and let live,' as long as no one is harming others is what needs to be embraced in this world."

"On this planet we are all the same, except for a few small differences, i.e.: skin color, religious background, culture, or sexual orientation. We all want love, peace on earth, and healthy happy children, who become healthy happy adults. We can only attain these things if we just respect each other and just live and let others live as well in peace and in harmony."

"Be respectful to all people including ones with special needs, and do this not because you feel sorry for them but because you know it to be the right way in human kindness and respect."

"I have always believed that we should always show respect to the families of our co-workers and friends, because by disrespecting them we are disrespecting our co-workers and friends. Soon we will have no more friends if this is the case. So always go above and beyond in this area and it will make for a more loving atmosphere and genuine relationships will be built out of this positive action."

Chapter 12

OUR TIME ON THIS EARTH AND OUR PURPOSE IN LIFE

Why are we here? What are we here for? What am I supposed to be doing with a life that may last to the age of 80, 90 or 100? How do I go from point A to point B and accomplish the things I am supposed to accomplish before my time on this earth is complete? How will I know that I have chosen the right path? The fact that our time on this earth can be limited, I believe we would want to get as much life in as possible and do all that we were meant to do before we are called back to Heaven.

What path am I supposed to follow? What causes am I meant to help fight? When is the passion for my life supposed to show itself and create spark in the lives I touch or can touch? Do I create it or was it there in the first place and all I had to do is just flesh it out?

Discovery is the operative word. We have to be the ones to discover it, create it, and help bring to fruition what our lives were meant to be. We are the ones that have to take the gift of life we have been bestowed by God, and help change lives and help change the world in whatever form we were meant to.

This I believe is our job and responsibility and the purpose for our lives is to help other people and to help change the lives of so many. This I know I believe is my role in this world and for so many with the same mindset. I believe just the way Michael Landon did on "Highway to Heaven," or Roma Downey on "Touched by an Angel," we were meant to in many instances to touch as many lives, spark interest and then leave them with an abundance they did not have before or knew they had. If in that time we are meant to stay with those we touch then perhaps a wonderful friendship has ensued and this makes for a wonderful life. We I believe want this for ourselves and will happily and joyously give it to others. The best part of ourselves is the part that we would want to show to the world and leaving all the negativity in a deep dark place that no one sees and we can rid ourselves of. We were meant to be the best people we can and should be.

Finding ourselves and becoming our authentic selves is what our true meaning should be. Just to exist on this planet with no purpose and to waste our lives is a sad life to one day just look back on and know the end is soon to come. So many of us just waste days and our time and we will one day look back and what we want to know is that our life meant something. We want to know that we made a difference in the lives of others for the better and in turn we will know that our life was well lived.

Our great President Abraham Lincoln once said: "And in the end, it's not the years in your life that count. It's the life in your years." There is so much to do and see in this world and there is only so much time allotted us. We must find where we want to go and be and take the journey. We will find the path we were meant to be led on, then soar. If indeed we have just this one life we need to make this one life shine with intensity and vibrancy.

We should shine with intensity and smile and breathe our true essence. What we need to become is our true selves, our authentic selves. When we find this and nurture it we will then be able to begin to discover who we are and what we can do.

God has put me here for a reason and it is not to just take up space, but to "become." I am here to learn and grow in the area God has placed me to be in which is helping others by giving donations to charity, volunteering, finding important causes such as homelessness and hunger and seeing what I can do and to use the power of the pen through my writing skills. I am here to change lives for the better and I know that by doing so I know that good will certainly come out of this. I know that I feel wonderful when I help people and I know they feel better as well.

We all feel good when someone shows they care about us, our well being. When we see someone elderly or infirm who cannot fend for themselves and we can assist them each in the end benefit, they feel good and we feel good. I know that is the way I feel and because I feel this way I want to live my life doing things that will help all groups of people and all kinds of people. Young and old alike and all in-between I believe I can make the world a better place by making the lives of each individual I meet a better life. I also remember that not all people want to be helped and we should only help out when asked to or when you know that helping is the best thing, because even the best of intentions doesn't work out all the time. But having the best intentions is always the best way to go and be.

Hopefully if we are raised well and had good parents, a good moral compass, and some good friends or teachers and learned well, we will discover our purpose and proper focus in life hopefully quicker that we might have otherwise.

Even if we didn't have those great parents, but had a mentor or teacher or one or more unfortunate life experiences that at some point brought us to a place where we realize that this is a place where I need to be then perhaps it might have been worth it. We don't want to have those terrible life experiences but sooner or later sometimes we do and in those times we can learn something about ourselves and the experience and perhaps it can lead us into the direction we were meant to be. As they say 'what doesn't kill us makes us stronger," and in doing so, these experiences teach us something that we can become stronger, wiser, much better human beings because of it.

I know in my own life, bouts of sadness and depression and feeling like everything in the world was bothering me and nothing good was happening; once I found the light at the end of the dark tunnel and turned it on, I realized that things would be okay. I learned that I should stop having the pity parties that we all go through and which no one after a short while wants to be a part of. I realized then, that there is a place in this world for me and I need to go there and be there and shine there.

What I found for me is that to become "a great writer," to become "a great humanitarian," is where my natural God given path lies, where I am meant to be. The writing ability is innate as well as my humanitarian feelings. I know that if I use them to the best of my ability they will come to fruition, like seeds planted in the ground, if watered, and nurtured, and cared for so many wondrous things will grow. From that beautiful growth we don't know what can happen or whose life we can affect in ways we cannot imagine. I want to be able to change lives, make others feel good and better about themselves. We all deserve to be happy and healthy both physically and mentally and it is my job to be a conduit for this in myself and others. Then we can pay it forward to others. This is something beautiful that should spread and if it does, it can be world-wide spread. World peace can only come if we begin the process, to change our lives first and then be the positive change that others see in us, so that they too can make changes in their lives.

    We don't need material things to make us feel good or make us feel like a whole person. The wonderful feelings that will make us whole is the helping of someone else.

    All the material luxuries we can buy cannot replace, peace of mind, good health, well being. A decent place to live, and with warmth and love and safety is important and we all want it and deserve it living on the earth. We do need money to survive, because without it we just won't survive. But if we care about others, and do things to create and make well this earth and its people, we are on the road to finding out who we are and what we are meant to do on this earth.

We have found our purpose and we will perform in that mode. The closer we come to this the happier, healthier people we will become.

I want to know that my life can and will be a conduit for peace of mind, love, friendship, joy, harmony and universal world peace for all. I cannot do it alone because we all need each other, but all of us together can fill those missing pieces to fit in that puzzle. I can do my share and perhaps someone else will see this and want to do it for the next person and pass it on and pay it forward as we all feel the happiness we were all meant to have in this world. Do we do enough? Sometimes we do and sometimes we don't. Can we always do more? Definitely!!!

"If our life ended today, tomorrow or a year from now, would we have lived our life to its fullest? Would we have made the right choices, helped as many people as we should or could have? Would we be able to leave this world having lived it as a man or woman who exuded peace and love, kindness and friendship to others? If the answer is no, reflect on your life now and start doing the necessary work to be in that realm of peace and love, kindness and friendship. Become the men and women that we need to become right here, right now. We want to one day if given the chance to look back and say we got it right in many more places then we got it wrong. When we are aware of what our lives are lacking or what areas need to be worked on we will do our very best to change things for the better. We were meant to shine and we will get there by becoming our highest and truest selves. Each day we should wake up and plan our day and what we can do to make it the best and brightest."

"Life is short!! We should work on not wasting our allotted time which is unknown to each of us, even though we all do it at times. We should make daily lists, life lists; discover important goals and dreams and work to see that they come to fruition."

"Pity parties only work for a short time and then we seem to be on our own. People want to help us but after a while of pity parties' people tend to feel the negative energy vibration that is surrounding us and for their own salvation need to part ways. But let go of the pity party and get involved by helping others or doing something proactive and then the positive energy will once again surround us. Once again people will join us at our "new party," and "will want to be," in our company and share time with us. So rid yourself of those "pity parties," and in place of them will be a "party of celebrations."

"Even though it can be difficult at times, try not to waste time. Time is precious and it can never be recovered or recaptured."

"Live in the moment (because this is all we have been promised). Many of us live in the past, many of us think about what might happen in the future and we then lose the meaning of right now; this second, this minute, this hour of day. It is all we have and we should be appreciative of this fact and live our lives accordingly."

"Living in the moment is the goal in life. Just remember that each of these moments are going to be memories one day. The goal is to create special lasting memories that we and others fondly look back on with family and friends. We are a very sentimental world and even though we must live in the 'now,' looking back is okay. The past may be gone, but the memories should not be forgotten and always cherished. The people that we knew that have past on want to be remembered as we would one day want to be remembered after we have passed on."

"Begin to question your purpose on this earth then continue to find the answers to your purpose and pursue them."

"Every phase of life takes us on a journey that we need to be on and places where we need to arrive at on our own individual journeys in order for us grow. So we need to embrace them, enjoy them and learn from them. Each place will give us new insight about ourselves that we did not have before and with this we grow and in time reach our highest selves."

"The only time to stop being opened to new experiences in this world is when we are gone. This idea should make sense. We are given a new opportunity each day to get it right and become opened to explore new opportunities. We should do our best to embrace them and make this life a great one."

"Our time with love ones here on earth is limited. So we need to make time with our parents, siblings, extended family members, including our friends. Because once this time is gone, there is no turning back. It is sadly over."

"When we look at life and our world, it is truly never about us all the time; it is also about other people. It is always about asking what I could do for others. How I can make a difference in the lives of others? It is not 'what can I get,' or 'what is in it for me.' It is about helping other people who co-exist with us. This is how we make our stamp in this world that will last posthumously."

"Positive loving thoughts and actions given to ourselves and to others will create a chain of positive loving people who pay it forward into the world. Do we not want a world that gives out positive energy instead of negative energy, good luck instead of bad luck, love instead of hatred, peace instead of war? When we give this out it comes back to us and it generates back out into the world and into the universe. Sometimes it is difficult, but we have to try. Giving someone a smile generates back something so wonderful. A good feeling inside for them and for us is generated too. We then begin to heal and we have in place good health instead of disease."

"Our time on this earth can be short or long, we just do not know when the sands of time in our own sand glass with run out. So, I believe we should strive to be the best people we can possibly be, help change the lives of others and help solve the earth's problems one person, one problem and with one action at a time. We need to always take time out to enjoy what life has to offer and it has so much. We need to love people, show generosity, and build a better world for the future generations. What we do with our lives will make a statement for all to see and hopefully admire while we are here and someday when we are gone."

"At any age we all want to be wanted, needed, respected, loved, and viable in someone's life. We need to matter to others and others need to matter to us. On an episode of, "The Partridge Family," a mother whose children had grown and left the nest made her feel no one needed her anymore. Eventually, when she felt someone such as a group of children did need her she felt rejuvenated and her life mattered again. This is what we all want at any age and we deserve to give it and to receive it. We need to matter."

"Time is a valuable tool of life. Once the day and some amount of the day is gone whether we have used it wisely or not it is gone for good. So we need to be consciously aware of our very own time and use it to the best of our ability. Sometimes we will get it right (using time wisely,) and sometimes we will miss the mark and fail (by wasting time.) But I hope we can learn from those failing moments and strive for the next time."

"Who are the 'real heroes,' in our lives? The first real Hero should be our 'Creator,' who made us in His Image. He should be looked upon as the first true Hero in our lives. Then our parents whether they are biological or adoptive who work hard to take care of us and love us should be looked upon as heroes as well. Our siblings, grandparents, aunts, uncles and those people who come into our lives to set the example of a good moral compass for us to live by can and are the real heroes in our lives as well. Movie stars, sports figures and celebrities are **not** the 'real heroes,' that we make them out to be, even though we may enjoy their performances. The real heroes in the world aside from the already mentioned are the policemen, firefighters, and others who help save lives. The courageous men and women who are fighting wars to protect us all; as well as scientists who spend years working hard to find cures for diseases that end lives far too quickly. Including the average man and woman who work hard to take care of their families are all 'heroes,' to the genuine definition. We need to re-examine who we define as heroes. Once we do we will appreciate the people that count the most for their accomplishments and not perhaps for what the media defines as fame, fortune, and popularity status as hero worshiping, because those things truly have no meaning when we look at our lives to realize what counts and what does not."

"We should always take time to enjoy the beauty that surrounds us, which includes the gardens, the sunsets, the trees, the people in our lives and all of God's children and animals that live with us in the universe. Spend time by yourself and reflect, spend time with others to create joyful memories and always give back to the universe."

Chapter 13

THE GIFTS AND STRUGGLES OF OUR LIVES

What are the gifts and struggles of our lives? If put on this earth sooner or later we will experience one of the many gifts and struggles of age, because no one is immune to either or, but if we pay attention we can learn from our struggles and grow stronger. We will then realize that the gifts in our lives will far outweigh the personal struggles we may face as we learn from them.

We will all have some struggles in this life because we cannot get to any age, whatever that might be, and not come away from any type of loss such as a loved one, the loss of a job, home, physical or mental disability and feel that life has been fair to us. Perhaps someone has done us wrong through some sort of betrayal or we learn through experience that life is difficult; with school and two jobs and raising a family. We have one hard knock after another and as we get up we get knocked back down again and it seems we have one bad thing after another happen to us.

There are some people in different parts of the world that have it far off worse then we do, with world wide hunger that never ends, homelessness where there is not shelter from the rain and snow and bitter cold, or the incredible heat of summer. There are laws where women are the property of men and will kill them if they do not obey their wishes. There are people with mental and or physical disabilities that are treated like lepers, these and so much more plague our world that we live in.

    Yes, some might say that we in America have people who suffer from homelessness and hunger, and where people struggle just to make ends meet. People face Cancer, and other horrible diseases and some may live through it and survive, while many do not and simply pass away. This can happen at any age, young and old and everyone in-between. Death and loss of life is never indiscriminate. If we are human then we face it.

    Probably the greatest gift would be to live to a ripe old age, healthy and with all our mental faculties in place and one night just pass away in our sleep. This would be the ultimate gift of life when it is our time to pass back from body into spirit and it is done with ease. This would be a blessing of all blessings. This may happen for some of us but not for most of us. We do not know how the wheel of fortune that spins will stop or when our number or time to go will appear. It comes without warning sometimes and everything that we may have started or tried to complete comes to a halt and is over and done with. Maybe someone with the same heart, mind and passion as us would continue the project we had set forth to make this world a better place, but if not then our work here is over whether complete or not.

But this I know for sure and believe in my heart, that if we live our lives doing what is right and in service to others, if we make it our business to be there for others in their time of need; our time will have been well spent when the end has appeared.

Love, kindness, respect, and compassion are important life attributes that we must imbibe in ourselves and teach to others. As long as we are not harming others physically or verbally we should live our own lives and become the best people we can possibly become. By living our own lives this way we then teach others. By becoming the example, others will hopefully learn and would want to follow this example.

But as we do live our lives both good things and bad occurrences do happen and we just need to accept this. We just need to change our thinking. We have to realize that life is not just filled with horrid days and loveless existence and death and destruction, but it can be filled with an over abundance of good outweighing the bad, peace overcoming war, light transforming the dark, and God and Love overcoming fear and pain.

Just think of this beautiful concept of a baby being born such as my two handsome nephews Jason and Matthew was for me, birthed by my loving sister Sherry. This happens to be the most profound blessing we could have been handed. He or she is the joy of the family and others who wish to enjoy this blessing from God above. We enjoy the smiles and sweetness a baby can bring and the hopes of a bright healthy future as they grow from boy to man and girl to womanhood. Our childhood is a wonderful time in life where we get to laugh, and play, and learn. It is a time where children believe in the angels and in rainbows, where life is in its purist form and we have a special innocence about ourselves. They say that the best time in a person's life is when we are a young child. Life was about having fun, laughing and about the joy of play. We didn't have any responsibilities which eventually could weigh on our hearts and minds. We do not realize this until we are adults with jobs and families and responsibilities of our own.

    I grew up with my mother and my sister. Unfortunately, my brother lived in another part of the world with our DNA father. But my sister and I had fun. We went to school, had our own friends and after school and on weekends hung out with them once our homework was complete. We watched our favorite shows on TV. We used our imagination to be creative without people telling us we were crazy to dream as we did or even fantasize. I remember loving the show Bewitched so much with Elizabeth Montgomery that I believed that how wonderful it would be to have magical powers just like hers or Uncle Arthurs. For one day all I thought about, is what I would do with those magical powers. With such believability in my head I imagined that I could pop in from one place to another, snap my fingers and my clothes would change and being able to levitate above people and listen in to their conversations without them knowing that I was there.

    As a young writer I loved using the playful side of imagination and create things which perhaps some people might call immature, but for being young, it did not matter, we were playing with our friends, expressing who we were and hopefully might be someday. We were just being ourselves.

    George Bernard Shaw once wrote: "youth is wasted on the young." I believe that we can always be "young," at any age. We just have to be willing to first believe that we are always as the saying goes "young at heart." If we express this innate happiness and fortune of being alive and being open to all that life has to offer we will all then feel and become youthful and filled with the effervescence light that is innate in all of us.

    The next part of our life is going through our teen years and into adulthood having to face the challenges of so many different life struggles and hope that along the way we don't forget to laugh and play and enjoy the important aspects of life.

Just remember that each phase of life is a gift we should "enjoy the process of." Enjoy the good to great ones and learn from the bad life experiences we all face from time to time.

I have gone from school to part-time jobs some I liked and others I dreaded and couldn't wait to find the next job, a better one that wouldn't be so awful. This is why school and learning is so important, with reading, writing and math and getting a good education is important. Life is tough enough and to not be able to speak with some form of intelligence than we are selling ourselves short and we won't get ahead except to only dead-end jobs.

We then fall in love, get married, have kids, and become so busy that we forgot about staying "young and hopeful," ourselves. We have constant busy lives with the kids and work and the kid's schedules. Life is constantly happening around us as we try to get things in order so we don't blow up and forget what truly is important in "the gift of life."

Before we know it the years are creeping up on us as we move from childhood to teen, to young person to full complete grown-ups. Ages 10-20 then to 30 then 40 and 50 and up and what we need to realize is, "they are just numbers." Yes as each year comes along we need not get depressed or saddened over a new age or decade of our lives, but be thankful and appreciative of the age that we do become. There are people for whatever God's reasoning are needed before what we on earth deemed far too soon. We could go at any age and time. We should be thankful that we are aging. We should appreciate each year and look for ways to make our lives well lived, by being of service to others and become creative and making a difference in the lives of others.

I hope that in my life I can be of service to others, through and by my words and by my actions. Perhaps in my writings I can say something that may resonate with someone in a more positive, healthy loving way and this in turn changes their lives to move forward, help themselves and perhaps pay it forward. In my actions I can help others by the giving of money and of the precious gift of my time to make the lives of others improved. Many people say that when you feel sad, lonely, or depressed and even bored, go "help someone." Helping makes both the recipient and the giver feel wonderful. It shows the less fortunate who we all can be one time or another that others do care and want to give back and help others. Because we never know when one day we could be the less fortunate one and would we not want others to be there for us.

As we age and get older, sometimes our bodies start to get weaker and for some because of being overweight, either type 2 diabetes becomes apart of some lives, or high cholesterol is a concern and watching our diets and exercising should become important. Our bodies' keep changing and our lives are not what they once were. We do not have the bodies we did as kids and we need to change our lives accordingly. With some and perhaps all of us eventually our bodies start to fall apart, but I am starting to believe that if in our young state, we do our best to take care of our minds and bodies that as we get older instead of falling apart our bodies will stay together as best as humanly possible.

This I believe will be due to both spiritual practice for our minds, and eating healthier and getting some exercise for our bodies. Our minds and bodies were given to us as a blessing to use, not abuse. Most times without realizing it we are abusing it and when instead we should be committed to taking care of keeping ourselves in a healthy state so we can enjoy our lives, the lives of others and do important things in this world. Because only when we do these things can we be alive and well to live "our best lives." When we are gone and our spirits move on the chance in this particular lifetime is complete.

I know for my lifetime that if I want to show others the way in their journey I have to have lived it in mine in order to show by example that we can overcome food or drug or any addiction that we might find ourselves in and which can turn our lives upside down.

In the end the gifts and struggles of our lives and life is to remember that we all have struggles and there are bad things going on in the world, internationally, nationally and even in our own back yards. But the true essence of our lives is that even with the struggles of age and all the difficulties age and life can bring, there is so much joy and happiness that can topple over all that pain. We should look at each day as the gift it was meant to be and be happy we are breathing without help and doing things for ourselves, if we have jobs and homes be thankful, if we have clothes on our backs and a few nice things know that this is great. Be thankful for them because they could disappear at anytime and even though it is our right to have these things, sometimes we could lose them due to no fault of our own.

So be happy and thankful for them; hope and pray that we do not lose them. As we get older and our health may decline and we may need medications and the costs become higher as the cost of living does and our paychecks and income stays the same on the lower end of the spectrum, life can and is tough.

    I am still a young man in my mid forties and feel good inside and out mentally and physically with an occasional problem. I have not advanced yet in age to the elderly stage. One day if I am blessed I hope to be there with all faculties intact and being able to enjoy the end part of my life as I did in the beginning and in the middle. But I do hope and believe that if I take care of all aspects of my life, my emotional and physical self as best as I can and do the right thing that all will hopefully turn out well. I will enjoy each day for the beauty it brings to me and billions around the world. I will learn to laugh, play and enjoy the beauty that surrounds me.

    We all need at any age to get back to the feelings of becoming and staying youthful. This way as we do age that each day is not a day that we wish to go back to sleep and not wake up whether for the rest of the day and not face life or go to sleep and not wake up at all.

    I believe "the gift of life," was meant to be lived as the gift it was intended. It was a blessing and is a blessing to be shared and lived by all. Even with the struggles of life, we have our birthdays, anniversaries, Thanksgiving, Christmas, New Years, and each religion and culture celebrating their own celebrations. If we focus on the wonderful things in this world and less on the bad, and take care of ourselves there will be more gifts for us and less struggles as we age. But as we take care of ourselves and enjoy our lives, we must not forget that there are bad things going on in the world and it is all of our responsibilities to help as much as we can to help others. We may not be able to solve all of the world's problems because they are much too big, but we can help "one person at a time," and "one world problem at a time." With this I know the gifts and struggles of our lives will be more "gift," and less "struggle." Amen.

"With luck we will all age and do it with grace, but age really is only a number. It's how we feel about love, life and the people that make us feel youthful and energetic. This is what it should be about. When we are not getting this then we need to re-examine our lives and see how we can change it for the better."

"The youthful part of us never leaves us. We just need to 'rediscover it,' and help nourish it and help it flourish. As we age we should enjoy, embrace, and be thankful for the gift of age and being alive."

"Bridge the gap as I have and become friends with an older person, they can have so much to teach us the younger generation if we embrace this concept and them and we will close the so called divide."

"We need to respect our elders; they have wisdom far beyond what we think we know."

"Our elders are the ones who were here before us and know so much more than we do, so by showing them respect, we are saying that I can learn from you, so that one day if we become blessed with the gift of age and become elders ourselves, we will know how to act and be able to teach the younger generations with confidence."

"Enjoy the gift of age because many people are not graced with this gift. So when you enter the 'zero,' ages, 20, 30, 40, 50 60 70 80 and beyond know we have been blessed with something that some people just do not get to attain and that is 'the gift of age.' If we look to this gift and respect it our lives will become the greatest it can possibly be. So remember: the achievement of age is a gift. Be gracious and embrace it if you've been blessed with it."

"Age and society should not dictate when a person should retire. Only the individual should decide, 'if and when,' they want to retire. We all need to flourish and grow and that means any age from babyhood until we pass on. Do not be the one to stop this growth for all who want to grow. If we want to work until we are 100 years of age we should be able to. We could be in the same boat one day and wouldn't want to be forced to have our voice be stilled or our actions stifled until we make the choice ourselves to stop enjoying what we enjoy doing. No matter if it is work, play or helping others, we should do it while it makes us feel joyous inside without people telling us otherwise."

"The meaning of each birthday should be that it is a gift of being alive, not an opportunity to think we are just getting older and nothing important is happening in our lives. If nothing is going on in our lives we should use each day to fix this problem and our life will be 'successful and full.' Then when our birthday does comes along we should enjoy it the same way a child looks forward to their birthday; as a time to have a party with presents, lots of fun and much good wishes bestowed upon us. This I believe is the significance of our birthdays."

Chapter 14

WITH LIFE, COMES THE SADNESS OF LOSS

In this beautiful world called earth that we call home while our spirits journey through this human experience, we will learn to encounter the heaven that we call "life," with its entire incredible splendor and we will encounter the hell, and pain called "loss of life," which is the other experience and side to life. We are born and given life which is a blessing and a gift to our families and through whatever circumstances we are born into, until life shows us differently, it is all we know to be true for us.

We all start out living with our families or guardians who hopefully will nurture and take care of us. We are vulnerable in their hands and need everything to be done for us for we cannot do much for ourselves for the first few years. If we are lucky we will have brothers and sisters, cousins, grandparents, uncles and aunts and a lot of the extended family which is prevalent in life. In the early stages of life if blessed we will have our parents do all the wonderful things for us that will make us happy and help us to grow in loving and healthy ways. They will clothe and feed us with wonderful meals they prepared and cooked with love. If lucky they hugged us and kissed us giving us a place to find solace in uncertain times and they gave us the stimulation to move forward. They will encourage us and make us feel appreciated and lucky to be alive even though in the early years we didn't know what that meant only that it felt good.

If we fall down and hurt ourselves they "kiss the boo boo," to make it feel better or if we bump our heads and the tears start to fall they will hold us, hug us and wipe away the tears and any pain we might experience. When as kids we play together and we fall and bruise or hurt ourselves our parents let us know we will be okay. A few minutes later it is all forgotten by us and we are playing with our friends again. If only as adults we could remember that when tensions flair and we should not think with our bruised egos, then life would be so much more loving for us all.

In this wonderful blissful time of life, we may see a grandparent or great grandparent who is in our lives and then one day is here no longer. We wonder what happened and don't realize that in this "life," there is also "loss." Children especially younger ones do not realize the concept of passing away and even us adults don't understand it or care to since passing away means the people whom we have loved and whom have loved us are no longer going to spend time with us on this earthly plane any longer. The life has ended and the body which has served its usefulness is no longer needed whereby letting the spirit go and returning it to heaven.

This concept is simple and easy to understand but so difficult to accept while we remain here on earth. This is loss and loss of any kind is filled with sadness, hurt and can many times lead to depression feeling we had lost the most important part of ourselves.

I believe as many do that we are just "spirits," on this earth having a "human experience," and that when it is our time to leave this world despite the fact whether we are ready or not, we must go and leave our bodies and return to spirit form. It is very difficult to understand however when young babies just getting started or children laughing and smiling and enjoying their lives can get taken from us and we just do not have a clue as to "why?"

We do not want to pass away at any time and we expect when we do get to that "certain age," we are pushed ahead in front of the line and we will go, and we hope it is in our sleep, peacefully fading back into spirit and not in some dramatic way. At that later stage and age in life we kind of expect it and can come to terms with it despite that fact that it will be hard to deal with when the time comes.

My mother had lost both her parents at a young age. First her dad, my grandfather, from Cancer at age 66 and her mother, my grandmother, at age 64, four years later due to an embolism in the brain which might have resulted sadly from her being hit by a car six months prior.

Both too young to die and leaving my mother with no parents and missing them both in times of her life she needed them the most. I think we always need our parents and loved ones so it is a devastating loss for all when death takes us. My sister and I lost the gift of having grandparents into the years when memories become stronger, more solid and more vivid. Even then we always remembered them and our experiences we had with them are ones we will never forget.

Sometimes we go in the middle years of our lives when we think things are going well and we are enjoying life and life is enjoying us. We find that all things are sincere bliss even with our good and bad days and then without a moment's notice a turn of events, dramatic or otherwise we too are taken and that loss too can be so painful for the ones we leave behind.

Sometimes we have to live with a disease and a turn of events leaves us in way that we no longer have the use of our arms and legs as did actor and activist Christopher Reeve. Plus, there are some who always go back and forth to their doctors or hospitals never seeming to get well. Some live in vegetative states, some live in war torn countries never knowing from one minute to the next if today is their last day. Some parts of the world live with floods, tornadoes and hurricanes such as the Tsunami in 2004, Hurricane Katrina back in 2005 or the Hurricane Sandy in 2012. Even though people have survived these horrific type occurrences, this too can be a sense of loss because of all these curveballs which make us wonder when this will end and when we will be able to live in better circumstances.

Sitting here writing this and knowing that I go through good days and bad days, I still am a very happy man who knows and counts the gifts and blessings I've been given. Though not rich monetarily, I am rich with so much of the important things such as good health, a home, a family and friends who I love and they I hope return that love. I know there are still others facing problems worse than I or you could ever dream or imagine. Knowing this we should do whatever we can to make the lives of others more meaningful and rich.

In this world there is "life and loss," and it can come at any time and at any age from inception of a fetus to an elderly person and to all of us in between. At the beginning there is "life," and at the end when we pass away there is "loss," to the ones we leave behind. We accept the world with both the good which are the "gifts," and the bad which are "losses." We hope we receive more gifts and are able to deflect the losses of any kind but we acknowledge that being upon this earth we will have to accept them both or else we cannot cope or survive. Many of the losses in this world are beyond our control unfortunately, but fortunately we all understand because we all have this in common. The greatest gift we do share is that we can, "help," each other get through it.

    The incredible experience of life is that we can help another person and in turn we feel good inside and they will as well. We can put a smile on our faces and we can go out into the world with happiness in our hearts. When we give thanks for all we have and do our best to make our lives the best we can we in turn give others the encouragement to make their life the best they can and only then will we benefit and experience the joy that life offers us. This I hope and believe will lessen the severity that loss in our lives can and will bring eventually. None of us will stay here forever and ultimately there is loss, but there is hope and promise and love and life that will get us through until it is our time to leave. If we help one another and give comfort to each other we won't extinguish, or outrun "loss," but we can find ways to cope, deal and go on making "our lives the best we can make it." Let "loss," be what it is, just a part of "life," but not the most important, even though it may feel like the saddest part. Celebrate life because Life is Good and God is Good…all the time. Amen.

"Experience, embrace, and show up for life. Be a participant in your own life and in the lives of others."

"Be enthusiastic about your life and helping other people become enthusiastic about their lives. Oprah says 'Live your best life,' and as I believe and continue this thought I say 'then teach and help others to live their best life,' by the example of living our own."

"No one knows why some of us have short lives; some of us are affected by disease, or have to live through one traumatic experience after another. It is the part of life that most times has no logical or sincere answers. We end up coming to the conclusion with the same question among many of 'why bad things happen to good people,' and that seems to have no answers. Life is just filled with both the good and the bad and we hope and pray the good outweigh the bad. Perhaps the best thing to do is try to live each day and bring our lives into the realm of our highest selves, even when sickness and sadness fill our days. We all have been given the 'gift of life,' with hopes and dreams, drama and struggles. Some lives seem to be going smoothly while others constantly get knocked down and after they get back up they end up back on the floor once again. What does life have to offer anyway except grief one might add who goes through the constant knock down mode? I pray only good come their way and the bad times and daily struggles retire, though I still believe that we need to live each day as successfully as we can. Look at that beautiful or handsome smile in the mirror, begin to tell ourselves that life is beautiful and our very own existence is beautiful and a blessing. In time we will believe it and our mind set of bad things happening all the time will begin to change. If we start to believe this, then each of us can be a positive force in our own world, and good luck will outweigh the bad, positive energy will replace the negative, hope replace sadness, health will replace disease, and life will return to the sweetness of its original form. Believe it and become it, become it and believe it, either way we must change our thinking toward LOVE and being a SOURCE OF LOVE for all the world and not a source of sadness."

"When you see a plane or helicopter soaring in the air wish them as I do each time one passes across the sky: 'Godspeed, angel blessings, peace, love, safety and Amen.' We should wish that their journey is a safe and peaceful flight and that they land and arrive safely. When I see a fire truck, ambulance, or police car in route with sirens blaring I wish them: 'Godspeed, angel blessings, peace, love, safety and Amen,' as well, that they get there in time to help save lives and that they are not too late. Time is of the essence and we should pray they get there in time. It could be one day that they would be coming to save us and we definitely want them to be there on time." Amen.

"When I enter a bus or a car, I pray 'Dear God, Archangel Michael, and Archangel Raphael: please bless this bus (or car) the driver, people getting on and getting off, all vehicles and all people surrounding us and let this be a peaceful, safe, loving journey for one and all, Amen.' I believe this prayer works and with that I feel safe." I wish the same for you too. Amen

"One of the most unfortunate life circumstances that many people around the world face are natural disasters. My heart and prayers go out to these people because I, or people I love could be in their place. I believe we should all pray for all the people and families who have lost their homes or lives, to earthquakes, tornados, floods, and terroristic attacks. I pray as well as for the people who are caught up in the wars for the only reason that they were in the wrong place or born into a family in a part of the world that wars are so prevalent. When I see this my heart becomes saddened. One reason I am saddened is because of all the human suffering added to the world that these natural disasters or terroristic attacks can produce. Including the uprooting of people who have lost everything except the shirts on their backs. When we see this we need to be thankful that those things are not happening to us because those people could be us. Pray for all of them, that they find peace, love, and a helping hand. That helping hand could and should be yours and mine. Sometimes we think we have so little what can we possibly offer to anyone else?" We just need to believe that every little bit helps and then once we do we would feel less helpless and then giving will become second nature. Then keep on praying and keep on giving more."

"Life is a gift we should embrace NOW. Because we are only promised this moment. Tomorrow is not promised to us and it may not come for us. The old saying 'Live each day as if it were our last,' is true. We should believe it and live it, this way there are no major regrets. If we do have some regrets and I am sure we all have some, they won't be the big ones, only small ones that will pass away in the wind."

"We all will leave this world one day and looking back on our lives we want to make sure we had lived it well, with integrity, respect and a willingness to help others and make a positive change in this world. We need to live from our hearts, and become the best people we can possibly become. It should be our life's goal that we see come to fruition."

Chapter 15

THE IMPORTANT THINGS THAT MATTER

"The important things that matter," should become our goal and life's purpose to discover what they are so we can make and give our lives and those around us the best possible life experience that we can. What I feel is important to me may not matter to you, because we are all individuals, with hopes, feelings, wants and desires that may differ. Even though ours may differ from each other we should all search within to find out what those are that belong to us and make them come alive.

I also think that the following may make sense to you as well as they do to me as starting points as we think about our own individual lives and what they mean to us and can mean to others:

- Giving and receiving love in all relationships and in all experiences

- Our families, friendships and all other relationships

- Our health, well-being and peace of mind

- Our jobs and livelihoods

- Living and working in safe and loving peaceful environments
- Living and working with and in integrity
- Remembering significant dates and times
- Volunteering and helping others
- Being creative and finding our inspiration
- Embrace Prayer, music, mediation and spiritual practice daily

There could be no greater divine life purpose, than to give & to receive love in all of our human relationships and experiences, starting within our own minds, which is where our thoughts begin, followed by what we say and then do, which will be the result or the effect of our individual and collective experiences. If we think about our lives from this level and remove any blocks such as what our egos (our small separated self) would try to convince us otherwise, it will be very easy for us to give and to receive love more easily. Giving and receiving love should be one of "the important things that should matter," to us for more profound living and loving one another.

I know for me what matters most is being a great son, brother and uncle in my family; a great caring friend to those gracious enough to include me in their circle of friends. I want to be a great worker and co-worker in the job which I make a living at; a great writer and a great humanitarian to the world living in my "divine life's purpose." I want to be able to live in a safe and loving home and peaceful environment as well as work in one. These are just some of what makes my life meaningful and purposeful.

Our families and friendships should be important to us and who we choose to spend our time with. Do we also not want to live in a home and work in a place that is safe, loving, and peaceful as well as a happy environment? Our jobs and livelihood are important because without them we cannot do the things that can create and fulfill our true purpose and calling, whatever that may be. Being healthy is probably the most important of many concerns in our lives. We can be the wealthiest people in the world and have all the riches money can buy, but if we are sick all the time and bedridden or cannot enjoy life's beauty, then being "rich," means nothing. If we do not have our health then we truly have nothing. We are truly "wealthiest," if we have our health, well-being and peace of mind. I pray for this gift for myself and I pray it for you the reader as well and our world.

As I wrote in an earlier chapter, it is important to

be a person of integrity. Otherwise no one can trust and believe in us, and perhaps why should they when we haven't given them cause to. If we live our lives with integrity, others can respect us and we can walk this world with our heads held up high. Wow! What a great feeling this is!

I know for myself and I would bet that others believe this too, that it is important to live life with a good moral compass. We should have a life with a sense of values that not always go with the crowd. I have always gone my own way, despite what others were doing around me. If young people my age did something I didn't approve of for myself I wouldn't go ahead and do it.

I never went with the crowd to please them or to be liked. I loved the sweet sounds and harmony of "The Carpenters," and "The Partridge Family," way after they were "in season," or "past their peak." If I didn't find other groups to be as good, I would stay with my favorites and not join the crowd. Therefore, I believe that we should find things that interest us and make us feel good inside and embrace them for what they bring to our souls and moods and spirits.

Finding charity organizations and volunteer programs as well as to send money and do what we can at any given moment is another "important thing that matters." As I have said many times, I have done so in the past, am doing some in the present and will do more in the future, to make someone else's life better. It is never about us, (most times,) it is always about the other person and how to make their life more meaningful and loving and more hopeful about what isn't going well in their life and what could be better.

When we take a look at the world at large we can see all the ills and problems that exist in the world. I believe we need to be a part that helps to fix as much as we can that is negative. I also believe that by helping to focus on "the important things that matter," in our lives and in the lives of others we can start to expand this into the outer universe. The important things that matter are ones where we take an inventory of what is working in our lives and what is not and then go about changing, fixing, making better what is wrong and acknowledging, accepting, embracing and cherishing what is working and continue to make it better still.

As old as the "human story," is, we all have great things going on in our lives and things that are not going well. We have things that we wish would never end and things that life will take away from us eventually against our will. As things go well for us on one hand, sometimes on the other hand we wonder when will these bad phases of our lives or difficult situations end. We hope, we pray, we love, we win, we lose, we gain, we console one another when we lose a loved one and laugh and sing and express happiness and joy when we celebrate a birthday or anniversary. We go through all the emotions a human has in our souls that express what we are feeling at any given moment in time.

Another important thing is finding a good community that respects our values and that inspires us to be the best we can be. They may be a religious or spiritual group, or reading group, or a group that loves to dance. Getting involved in a community of like-minded people I think is important. Sometimes it is sad when we don't even know our own neighbors, me included in the way it really counts. The days of "Donna Reed," where we know our neighbors and are friendly and caring of them and them to us seem to have left our embrace. We now have become people who live next door to blank faces, unknown people, uncertain of their names and what they represent in the world. I too feel that way with my neighbors. If I pass them as I leave for work or come home from the store I will most certainly say, "Hello, and how are you?", Or perhaps, even a wave that speaks hello. We cannot just ignore our neighbors though many of us do.

I believe and hope that becoming better neighbors and friends in our community we can put forth "the important things that matter," into better focus where we all should be and would want to be.

I think another of "the important thing that matter," is to be creative in some way. To draw, to write, paint, sculpt, dance, engage in arts and crafts, or whatever you think can be a force to do good and inspire others to also become creative is important. If we use our energies to create good and love into this world it will be returned to us and inspire others to go the same way. With these positive energies going out into the world we would start to eradicate war and illness, hunger and homelessness or any pain and suffering. We would replace it with abundance of every kind with peace and joy along with it.

I truly believe as well that to bear a more fruitful existence, we should and must embrace and include the following: prayer, music, meditation and spiritual practice each and everyday of our lives. Doing something that will rejuvenate the spirit is so vitally important and necessary for us to survive and thrive in this life which at times can be so dispiriting and can bring us down. However we must bring ourselves back up and bring others with us and I know in my heart, prayer, music, meditation and some sort of daily spiritual practices will bring us there. I want this for my life and I want it for your lives as well. I want us all to attain inner peace and harmony within our minds and within our hearts as well. We must listen to that little small voice for God inside of us and He will lead the way.

So I believe for my life and I hope for those lives who live in the world with me that by looking and examining "the important things that matter," to each of us and applying it we can inspire one or two other people who would do the same and change their life and change other lives for the better, and if so "what a wonderful world," this would and can still become for all of us to live in and enjoy in LOVE....Namaste and Amen.

"If we take care of our health our time on this earth will increase with abundance, if we ignore our health concerns our time on this earth may be shortened. As I worked in a doctor's office this male patient was in such a hurry to have his test performed and head back to work. The fact that he had to wait bothered him. The test like all tests are important and I told him to hold on a while longer; he'll get his test done and be on his way back to work. I let him also know, 'he needed to take care of his health or his job wouldn't mean much.' Our time on earth is limited enough, so doing what we can to increase it is the best way to live."

"Remember the birthday, and anniversary of family and friends as well as people who don't expect it. It can sometimes be a double edged sword if you do forget, but still be the one who remembers. That special day will mean a lot to the ones you remember, so write them, call them and let them know you care."

"Be a creative person: write, draw, paint, dance, do photography, or make a quilt for someone. Being creative expresses positive energy into the world. It encourages others to find their creative energy force and this action alone makes for a healthier universe."

"Always remember that no matter what problems we have, and all of us do have problems, some large and some small, and somewhere in the middle, there is always someone out there in this big vast complicated world whose problems are worse and deeper than ours. This doesn't say that our problems are unimportant; it is only for us to realize that there are other people in the universe who are suffering more than we can imagine. As we pray for our problems to be healed, pray for others to heal their problems and to find peace and ease in their struggles as well. When we pray for others to heal, we too will receive a healing from God and the universe, which is the blessing of giving and receiving."

"Some of our holidays sometimes lose their true meaning and essence and we just see it as a day off to sleep late, have a BBQ, or go to the stores for sales. It is so important that we always remember and acknowledge what these holidays really represent. Memorial Day and Veterans Day are days to remember the people who either fought and lived or have died in wars to save and protect the rest of us and we must never forget these brave men and women. Dr. Martin Luther King Jr. Day, is to remember the long fight on bringing all the races together and the long struggle ahead that we all still face. He taught us that we should want to live together in peace and harmony. Labor Day is a day to respect the working men and women for all our hard efforts in trying to earn a living for ourselves and our families. Thanksgiving is one day among the other 364 days to give thanks to all that we have. Parents, teachers, and mentors should teach the children about these and other important holidays so that they will grow to know that holidays have much more significance than many people give them credit for."

"Always look for the rainbow after the rains have finished descending. The rainbow is a rebirth of life. It expresses a better and brighter today and all our tomorrows. It is a representation of what we want our lives to become and that of others as well."

"Some of my favorite words, thoughts, ideas, and concepts that I hope I exude and express to others through my actions are: Love, friendship, kindness, compassion, being supportive, caring, peace, and harmony. If sometimes through life's struggles I have fallen short, then I have work to do to genuinely exude those ideas and concepts to others. Hopefully they can be yours or you can find ones that express the essence of who you are. But in the end, be the embodiment of all that which is LOVE. The Love of God, the love of the angels both on earth and in heaven, love for the universe and the earth, love for ourselves, all of humanity and life forms as we know. Giving and receiving love which is what we were born to express will make all our today's and tomorrows richer. I want that for you as much as I want it for myself and may we live it joyfully…Amen."

EPILOGUE

In this one life we have to live, I feel as I live my own is that we should be kind, caring and decent people. We need to be caring to ourselves first and then for other people as well. Whether it is a family member, friend, co-worker, neighbor, stranger at the grocery store or anyone we meet on our own travels as we walk the globe, we need to be the best we can for all people that we meet. We are kind and caring to the people that we know, but it says something about a person if they are kind to strangers, people who we have no invested interest in and may never see again. This I believe is what makes a "good," person, "great." We all have the capacity for "greatness," if we so choose.

Our world is filled with smart people. We truly have enough of "these," types of people. What the world finds in short supply but does exist and which needs to come to the forefront are compassionate and caring people. People who would want to make a difference in the lives of others. People who are not out for personal gain, fully and completely. The "short," supply of people who are compassionate and caring are certainly out there. If we go to any soup kitchen, or homeless shelter, or place where there is a need for human kindness, people will rise to the occasion and be there to help all who need a helping hand and a smile to light up their sad face. We need to include a few kind words to encourage better feelings about one who may not feel worthy and here we are doing what we have been "chosen," to do in this life which is to change lives for the betterment of humanity.

There is so much negativity and evil floating, living, breathing and existing in the world that we must be the ones to combat it and change it. "Good must triumph over evil," as the saying goes and we must be the ones to put "goodness and blessings," out into the universe. We must be the ones that put love and peace and hope back out into the world so that evil and black despair dissipate and go back into nothingness and all that is its opposite shine upon us and our world instead.

As we who are "spirit," live on this planet in this earthly form known as the "human experience," only do so but for such a short time. If we only live here for such a short time, why would we not want our world to be a place filled with loving kindness for all of us? In this world would live health and happiness, joy and laughter and we could live and work in peaceful, harmonious surroundings. I believe what we give out we will receive back. If we give love and friendship it will be returned to us. If we give out pain and sadness and attack others, we will receive it back as well.

Even if no one has attacked us back we might feel in some way like they did because of how we un-lovingly treated others.

What I hope for is that we all join forces so we can have the "good," float back out into this world and spread to each and every one of us. Maybe we can cultivate peace and joy, happiness, laughter and loving tenderness. May it flood back into the world where it belongs. It must always start with you and me. When we do this others will see and feel the positive loving vibes we possess and give out which in turn will then give others permission to be more loving and kind as well to all those they meet. When we all do this, so will we all benefit.

We live in a world that when it comes down to it, we are all we have and we need to take care of one another, period. We need to support each other, completely and fully. If we give to others our compassion and care, then we are on our way to "healing." I like to call it **"OUR SMALL CONTRIBUTIONS TO THE HEALING OF THE WORLD."** We must always be there for others. It is the best gift we can give others and that is **"THE GIFT OF OURSELVES."** I do it in my life and world and hope that others will do it in their life and world as well.

The end result is a more loving and blessed world for you and for me and for each other. The peace we wish to see in this world will come to fruition one day but we must be the ones to cultivate it and be the conduits for it and tend to our parts of the garden so we can bring beauty back into our world in all places across the globe. Let each of us do our part and what we will see is a beautiful world garden that has lovingly blossomed for all of us to rejoice in. **LETS START TODAY!!!! HEY, START RIGHT NOW AND MAKE YOUR LIFE MATTER!!!!** God bless us all, angel blessings, peace, love and so it is we all say...Amen.

THANK YOU FOR READING MY BOOK!!!!!

I'M FOREVER THANKFUL AND GRATEFUL!!!!!!

PLEASE WATCH FOR MY NEXT BOOK COMING SOON..."HOW TO HEAL THE WORLD, BY HEALING OURSELVES FIRST." THANK YOU

ABOUT THE AUTHOR

Joel Dex Goor is a first time book author. Joel wants to help others through his teachings on how to become better people. He earns his living working as a Para-Professional in the New York City School System with Special Needs children, as he likes to call it, "THE HELPING AND HEALING PROFESSION." He gives the students his compassion and genuine concern for their well-being. This is where his love for humanity is put to work. His passion is to help others, and write about humanity and how we can become the best within ourselves and then extend it outward to our world. Joel would like to lecture, become a motivational speaker and a life coach.

He has finished his first complete book and proud of it entitled "YOUR LIFE IS A BLESSING...SO LIVE IT THAT WAY!!!" He has written over 40 writings which include poems, prayers and essays which he has published on his blog entitled: "My happiness, gratitude and appreciation blog.com," to touch the heart and move the spirit.

Joel also has over 1900 'LIKES' on his fanpage on FACEBOOK "MY HAPPINESS, GRATITUDE AND APPRECIATION PAGE."

Joel welcomes you to view and join his new website: "YOUR LIFE IS A BLESSING SO LIVE IT THAT WAY.COM." Joel wants to continue writing and create pieces that speak to humanity's soul and spirit and to re-awaken the light in people who thought it lost.

In his spare time he loves to watch the classic movies on TCM and classic sitcoms on DVD. He loves reading books on or hearing talks on the spiritual realm, books on angels, on spiritual thinkers that want to change the world for the better, such as Marianne Williamson, Doreen Virtue, and Oprah Winfrey among others.

Joel wants to join that group of "NEW SPIRITUAL THOUGHT, THINKERS AND SPEAKERS" and become an extension of the past great thinkers as well as the current ones that live and speak in our world today. Joel is currently working on his second book "HOW TO HEAL THE WORLD, BY HEALING OURSELVES FIRST." Joel is devoted to his loving family and friends who help sustain him. Joel resides in Brooklyn NY.

www.ingramcontent.com/pod-product-compliance
Lightning Source LLC
LaVergne TN
LVHW051113080426
835510LV00018B/2008